DOG DAYS
and
DANDELIONS

DOG DAYS
and
DANDELIONS

A LIVELY GUIDE TO THE ANIMAL
MEANINGS BEHIND EVERYDAY WORDS

Martha Barnette

St. Martin's Press
New York

www.stmartins.com

Library of Congress Cataloging-in-Publication Data

Barnette, Martha.
    Dog days and dandelions : a lively guide to the animal meanings behind everyday words / Martha Barnette.—1st ed.
        p. cm.
    ISBN 0-312-28072-6
    1. English language—Etymology—Dictionaries. 2. Zoology—Nomenclature (Popular). 3. Animals—Terminology. 4. Animals—Folklore. 5. Figures of Speech. I. Title.

PE1583 .B37 2003
422—dc21   2002036752

First Edition: February 2003

10   9   8   7   6   5   4   3   2   1

For Kate Torp,
who also loved to learn

The etymologist finds the deadest word to have been once a brilliant picture. Language is fossil poetry.

—RALPH WALDO EMERSON

INTRODUCTION

Animals lurk everywhere in our language—if only you know where to find them. There are the obvious examples: We refer to a brief snooze as a *catnap,* and we use the term *dog-eared* to describe the turned-down page of a book. But hundreds of other animals lie hidden in words we use every day. These creatures are harder to see, because they're covered in linguistic camouflage, and concealed in surprising places. There's a small horse inside the word *tacky,* a leggy bird in *geranium,* a female sheep in the name *Rachel,* a pig in *porcelain,* a shrew in *shrewd,* an infestation of bugs in *lousy* and *grubby,* and a pony to be straddled in *bidet.* But to uncover these and other animals hiding inside familiar words, it takes a little etymological sleuthing.

The word *sleuth* is a case in point. A few hundred years speakers of English used the term *sleuthhound* as a synonym for "bloodhound," a breed of dog distinguished by its keen sense of smell and ability to focus intensely while sniffing out its quarry. The first part of the word *sleuthhound* derives from an even older term that means "track" or "trail." By the nineteenth century, English speakers had begun shortening the animal name *sleuthhound* to *sleuth,* and applying it to equally dogged human investigators.

Words like sleuth, as well as hundreds of others, have a great deal to tell us, not only about our relationship with animals, but also about ourselves. Words, after all, are a kind of linguistic fossil record, preserving vivid images of the many ways throughout history that humans have observed, admired, feared, hunted, domesticated, befriended, trained, studied, and eaten our fellow creatures.

As I noted in my previous books, *A Garden of Words* and *Ladyfingers and Nun's Tummies: A Lighthearted Look at How Foods Got Their Names,* the study of word origins provides a wonderful means of backing into all sorts of fascinating information about history, science, culture, language, and mythology—and in a way that's not only enlightening, but entertaining. In the pages that follow, we'll uncover the startling images of animals scattered throughout the English language: the caterpillar in your *chenille* bedspread; the gassy little dog that inspired our word *feisty*; the bird beak inside your tailbone, or *coccyx*. Along the way, we'll uncover parts of other animals embedded in familiar terms, such as the goat horn in the word *cornucopia* and the deer innards in the expression *humble pie.* We'll take a look at a few mythical beasts inside other English words, like the many-tongued monstrosity that inspired the word *blatant,* and we'll meet a few animals, like the *porpoise* and *hippopotamus,* that have other animals' names nestled inside their own.

In addition, we'll consider several less familiar but nevertheless useful words that also have animals inside them. (After all, if someone describes you as *scombroid,* or calls your clothing *chatoyant,* won't you want to know whether you've been complimented or insulted?) Finally, we'll discover the answers to such timeless questions as "What is a *snollygoster*?—and why shouldn't we elect one to public office?" and "Is there a specific word for badger poop? What about otter droppings?" (Yes and yes. See *crottin.*) And "Which language has the most colorful and picturesque name for the @ symbol?" (Hint: It's not English. For a long list of other languages' amusing animal names for this symbol, check out the entry on *cochlea*.) I've also included a few terms with animals hiding in plain sight—like *dog days* and *swan song*—because the stories behind them are so interesting.

As you've probably surmised, this book is quite dense with information. Rather than try to read it straight through, you might want to think of it as a browsing book. Come to think of it, the word *browse* itself is yet another that contains an animal image. Etymologists suspect that the word *browse* derives from a much older French noun that means "a bud" or "young leaf." Originally, speakers of English used the verb *to browse* to indicate the manner in which goats, deer, and cattle go moseying about, taking their time as they eat, nibbling at whatever buds or leaves look particularly inviting. Only later did our word *browse* acquire its modern sense—that of leisurely wandering the pages of a book and pausing to savor whatever catches your eye.

So, browse away—and happy sleuthing!

DOG DAYS
and
DANDELIONS

A

The first letter of our alphabet has an "ox" in it. The letter *A* goes all the way back to the first letter in the ancient Semitic alphabet, which was apparently adapted from an Egyptian hieroglyphic. In Hebrew, this first letter was called *aleph,* which literally means "ox." Scholars believe the earliest versions of this letter may have looked more like an inverted *V* with a bar across it, perhaps symbolizing the horns on an ox's head. The Phoenicians later simplified the Semitic letter and turned it on its side. The Greeks adapted the letter further, calling it *alpha.* The Romans borrowed this ox-inspired letter and gave it its final form. Actually, the letter *A* isn't the only one with animal origins. See **C**.

AARDVARK See LOBSTER.

ADULATION

When the ancient Romans used the verb *adulari,* they were alluding to the enthusiastic wiggle of an eager-to-please puppy. In its earliest sense, *adulari* literally meant "to fawn over someone like a dog wagging its tail." Over time, this word's meaning expanded to include the more general notion of "to flatter in a servile fashion." As early as the eighteenth century, speakers of English were using a descendant of this word, *adulate,* to mean "admire or praise excessively," and its noun form, *adulation,* for "excessive admiration or flattery." See **FAWN.**

AEGIS

Usually pronounced "EE-jiss," the word *aegis* means "protection," "patronage," "guidance," or "controlling influence." (As in "The all-day seminar, 'Undergarments of the Ancient Babylonians,' will be presented under the aegis of the Classics department.") The source of the word lies in classical mythology, where the ancient Greek term *aegis* could denote either the mighty shield of Zeus or the breastplate of Athena, which bore the dreadful visage of the snake-headed Medusa, the Gorgon who turned to stone anyone who dared to gaze upon her.

Most authorities believe that the Greek word *aegis* derives from an earlier Greek word, *aix,* meaning "goat." The reason: in antiquity, people often made shields out of stretched goatskin. This idea of an *aegis,* or a goatskin shield, performing a protective function expanded to include a more abstract sense as well—that is, providing the auspices under which something occurs. (In fact, see **AUSPICES.**)

AERIE

Today the word *aerie* denotes "an elevated and often secluded dwelling," as in "Harry and Mary and their canary Larry live in an airy *aerie* near Glengarry." In its original sense, however, the word *aerie* referred to a "the nest of a bird of prey built in a high place, such as that of an eagle or a hawk." This word is pronounced either "AIR-ee" or "EER-ee," and is sometimes spelled *eyrie*. English speakers modeled *aerie* after the French word *aire*, which denotes such a "nest," or more generally "a flat, open space." The connection between the two is the fact that eagles sometimes make their nests on a flat space high on a rocky cliff. The source of the French *aire*, however, isn't entirely clear, though it may derive from the Latin word *area*, meaning among other things, "a piece of level ground" or "threshing floor." (For another animal word involving a threshing floor, see HALO.)

AIGRETTE

Pronounce it "ay-GRETT" or "AY-grett," but any way you say it, an *aigrette* is a spray of jewels usually worn in the hair or on a hat. English speakers borrowed this bird word directly from French, where the term *aigrette* is the name of the etymologically related egret, a bird whose head sports a similarly shaped plume. If you want to get really fancy, you can also correctly apply the name *aigrette* to the feathery top of a dandelion—a weed that, incidentally, has a name that commemorates another animal entirely. See DANDELION.

AILUROPHILE

An *ailurophile* ("eye-LOOR-uh-file") is a "cat-lover." It's from the Greek word for cat, *ailuros*. It's sometimes spelled *aelurophile*, in which case it is pronounced with an initial "ee" sound. An *ailurophobe*, on the other hand, is someone who suffers from a morbid fear of felines, as in "Isn't it funny how they always seem to insist on climbing into the lap of the one person in the room who's an ailurophobe?" See **CHATOYANT**.

ALBATROSS

With a wingspan of up to twelve feet, the huge sea bird known as the *albatross* can use sea breezes to glide for hours at a time, coming ashore only to breed. Because of this bird's remarkable size and its ability to remain aloft for so long without flapping its wings, sailors long believed that the albatross possessed magical powers, and that harming one brought bad luck.

This superstition is at the heart of Samuel Taylor Coleridge's 1798 poem "The Rime of the Ancient Mariner," in which a mariner cruelly kills an albatross while onboard a ship near Antarctica. Shortly afterward, the wind dies down and the ship is stuck at sea. Angry crewmen blame the mariner and hang the large, dead bird around his neck in retribution. "Instead of the cross, an albatross / About my neck was hung." The image of this heavy load around one's neck has become a metaphor for any seemingly unshakable burden, guilt, or worry.

The roots of the name *albatross* apparently lie in the term sixteenth-century Spanish and Portuguese sailors used for another sea bird, the pelican. They called this bird an *alcatraz*— a name possibly deriving from an Arabic term meaning "the diver." Seafaring Englishmen borrowed this name, variously spelling it *alcatras* and *alcatrace*. They also mistakenly applied it to the large ocean-going bird whose name eventually morphed into *albatross*.

The term *albatross* also appears in golf, where it refers to a score of three strokes under par on a hole, or *double eagle*. The use of *albatross* for such a three-strokes-under score arose by analogy

4

with other ornithologically oriented golf words, such as *birdie* ("one stroke under"), *eagle* ("two strokes under"), and *buzzard* ("two strokes over").

And the small, rocky island in San Francisco Bay called *Alcatraz*? The name of this famous prison site is indeed thought to derive from a preponderance of pelicans there.

ALCATRAZ See ALBATROSS.

ALOPECIA

Alopecia (pronounced "al-uh-PEE-shuh)" is the medical term for baldness or hair loss. It derives from the Greek word *alopekia,* or literally, "fox mange"—because foxes often suffer from that skin disease. (For another foxy word, which also happens to be a distant relative of alopecia, see VULPINE.)

ALYSSUM

The popular garden plant *alyssum* is lovely to behold, but a rabid animal snarls inside its name. The word *alyssum* derives from the ancient Greek term *ályssos,* which means "curing canine madness," a combination of *a,* meaning "not," and *lýssa,* a word for rabies that may go back even further to an ancient root meaning "wolf-ness." If so, this would make alyssum a distant linguistic relative of another wolf-word, *lycanthropy.* See LYCANTHROPY.

The reason behind this frightening flower name: For centuries, people believed that this plant could cure rabies. (The same belief is reflected in alyssum's English synonyms, *madwort* and *heal-*

dog.) The Greek word *lýssa* also inspired the English flower name *antholyza,* so named because its blossom resembles the gaping jaw of a rabid dog.

Actually, a form of the Greek *lýssa* also survives today in the modern veterinary word *lytta,* which refers to the thin, cartilaginous strip on the underside of a dog's tongue. The ancients thought this structure was a parasitic worm that left dogs vulnerable to rabies, and that surgically removing this "worm" during puppyhood would make dogs immune to the disease. (The dubious nature of this prescription is reflected in Samuel Johnson's always entertaining *Dictionary of the English Language,* published in 1755. Johnson defines the expression *to worm* this way: "To deprive a dog of something, nobody knows what, under his tongue, which is said to prevent him, nobody knows why, from running mad.")

ANSERINE

If you want to describe someone or something that is goose-like, the word *anserine* will do just fine. Pronounced either "AN-suh-ryne" or "AN-suh-rinn," the word derives from the Latin for goose—*anser*—a distant relative of *gander*. These words are also relatives of the name for a type of duck that dives for fish—*merganser*. This bird's name is a combination of *anser* and the Latin word *mergere,* meaning "to plunge," which is also a relative of *merge* and *submerge.*

ANTHOLYZA See ALYSSUM.

ANTHURIUM

This flower's name was inspired by the distinctive "tail" that droops from the middle of its brilliant, heart-shaped bract. *Anthurium* is a combination of the Latin stems *anth-* meaning "flower," and *-urium,* meaning "tail." (For another Latin "tail" word, see PENCIL.)

The *anth-* in anthurium is a linguistic relative of several familiar words, including *chrysanthemum,* or "golden flower," as well as one of the loveliest words in the English language, *anthology.* Literally, an *anthology* is "a gathering of flowers"—a literary bouquet, in other words—that takes its name from the Greek words *anthos,* or "flower," and *legein,* "to gather." The *-urium,* or "tail" in *anthurium,* meanwhile, also wags inside several other English words, including *arse* (and its American English variant, *ass*), as well as the doggy word *cynosure.* See CYNOSURE.

ANTIPELARGY

The rare but lovely word *antipelargy* is a bird word that is certainly worth reviving. It comes from the Greek word *antipelargia,* meaning "mutual love," but take a closer look at this word and you'll see the faint outlines of a pair of devoted birds looking after each other.

The word *antipelargia* derives from the Greek *pelargos,* meaning "stork," a bird the ancients considered especially affectionate. (In this case, as sometimes happens in Greek, *anti-* connotes the idea of "in exchange for," rather than "against.") In 1656, an English glossary defined *antipelargy* as "the reciprocal love of children to their parents, or (more generally) any requital or mutual kindness." A later text defined it as "a mutual thankfulness or requital

7

of a benefit; but especially a child's nourishing a parent in old age." In any case, *antipelargy* is a word—and an idea—that deserves wider use. (For another stork word, see **PELARGONIUM**.)

APIAN

If you want to describe someone or something as being "like a bee," whether in terms of appearance or industriousness, the word you want is *apian*. [(As in "Um, I can't tell if this is a typo—did you mean to say the new employee is 'apian' or 'a pain'?")] Deriving from the Latin word *apis,* meaning "bee," *apian* is a relative of *apiculture,* the keeping of bees, and *apiary,* a place where bees are kept.

The Greek word for bee, however, comes from an entirely different linguistic family and is the source of a popular feminine name. See **MELISSA**.

APRINE

If you wish to compare someone to a boar, try using the term *aprine*. It's a rare word, but serviceable, as in "Not only was Vanessa's most recent date a bore, he was positively *aprine*." The term derives from the Latin word *aper,* meaning "wild swine," and is a relative of apricide ("the slaughter of a wild boar"), as well as the masculine name *Everett*. See **EVERETT**.

AQUILINE

Most often applied to a nose that is curved or hooked like an eagle's beak, the adjective *aquiline* derives from Latin *aquila,* which means "eagle." *Aquiline* is also used more generally to describe anything "having eaglelike characteristics." From the same bird word comes the Spanish surname, *Aguilar*.

ARI

The masculine name *Ari* comes to us courtesy of the Hebrew word *ari*, meaning lion. Similarly, the name *Ariel* comes from Hebrew words that mean "lion of God." (For more lion names, see LEO.)

ARIEL See ARI.

ARNOLD

The name *Arnold*, and its French variant, *Arnaud*, literally means "strong as an eagle" or "eagle-ruler." Both derive from the Old High German words *arn*, meaning "eagle," and *wald*, meaning "power."

AROUSE See ROUSE.

ARCTIC

The ancient Greeks' word for north was *arktikos*, a name that literally means "of the bear." The reason: the Greeks associated this direction with the most prominent constellation in the northern sky, the (vaguely) bear-shaped set of stars now referred to a *Ursa Major* (Latin for the Great Bear). In fact, the Greek word for bear, *arktos*, and its Latin counterpart, *ursa*, derive from the same prehistoric root. See URSINE.

ASININE

This word for stupid, silly, or stubborn derives from Latin *asininus,* literally meaning "asslike"—a reference to a donkey's obstinancy and presumed lack of intelligence. (The backside type of ass, by the way, is a variant of the English word *arse,* which goes back to an ancient root for tail.)

Asinine, incidentally, is a linguistic cousin of the "beast of burden" that supports a painter's canvas—see **EASEL.**

AUSPICES

In ancient Rome, the *auspex* was a state official whose job was to predict the future by observing the behavior of birds. The name *auspex* (and its plural, *auspices*) is a descendant of the Latin word for bird, *avis* (a relative of such words as *aviation*), and *specere,* "to look at," from which come several other words involving "looking," including *spectacle, perspective,* and *conspicuous.*

Whenever the Romans faced an important decision, they made sure to consult these professional bird watchers, or *auspices,* who would study the flight, chatter, and feeding of birds for clues that would help them foretell the future. The service that these *auspices* provided was known as an *auspicium,* a term that eventually came to refer to the good or bad omens themselves.

Occasionally speakers of English now use the word *auspice* to mean "observation of and prophesying based on the actions of birds," also known as *ornithoscopy* (pronounced "oar-nih-THOSS-kuh-pee"). More often, however, we use the word *auspice* to mean any kind of omen, especially a favorable one. This favorable sense of *auspice* also remains in our phrase *under the auspices of,* which implies the presence of some sort of benevolent protection and guidance. Similarly, an *auspicious* debut is a promising one—regardless of what any feathered fortune teller might say. See AEGIS.

AVIATION

Just as the invention of the airplane was inspired by the flight of birds, the word *aviation* itself has its origins in the Latin word for "bird," *avis*. This makes *aviation* a linguistic relative of such words as *avian*, meaning "of or pertaining to birds," and *aviary*, a "place where birds are kept." See AUSPICES.

AZTEC

The name of the *Aztecs* derives from that of a leggy bird and commemorates the legendary site in Central Mexico where the Aztecs supposedly originated. This place was called *Aztlan*, a name that in Nahuatl, the Aztecs' language, literally means "the place of the herons," from the Aztecs' word for "heron," *aztatl*.

BAT ONE'S EYES

There's an animal moving around inside this phrase, but not the one you might expect. The *bat* in this case alludes to a term from falconry, one that refers to the action of a hawk rapidly beating its wings. As a 1615 falconry manual puts it, "Batting, or to bat, is when a Hawke fluttereth with her wings either from the pearch or the man's fist, striuing as it were to flie away."

This "bat" is a variant of the word *bate,* a descendant of the Latin word *battuere,* that means "to beat." Thus the phrase *to bat one's eyes* is an etymological relative of such "beating" words as *beat, battle,* and *abate* (originally, "to beat down," then later "decrease").

And the leathery-winged, nocturnal animal we call a *bat*? The name of this vespertilian creature is an alteration of the Middle English term for it, *bakke,* which in turn was adapted from a similar-sounding Scandanavian name. See **VESPERTILIAN**.

BATRACHIAN

The adjective *batrachian,* which means "pertaining to frogs or toads," comes from the Greek word for frog, *batrachos.* Oliver Wendell Holmes once put this adjective to fine use when he

wrote of "the batrachian hymns from the neighboring swamp."
And if you're you're afraid of frogs, you're said to be afflicted with
batrachophobia.

You never know when you might need a word for "a battle
between frogs and mice"—well, *do* you?—but you'll be ready
with the word *batrachomyomachy*. Pronounced "BAT-ruh-koh-
mye-AH-mah-kee," this English word is adapted from the Greek
word *Batrachomyomachia*, the title of an ancient poem. No one
knows who wrote it, although some attribute it to Homer. Presented in the style of heroic epics like *The Iliad*, this comic work
chronicles a conflict in which mice are nearly overwhelmed in a
bloody battle against ferocious frogs, until the gods intervene and
send in the crabs as reinforcements.

This term for "a battle between frogs and mice" derives from
the Greek words *batrachos*, meaning "frog," *mūs*, "mouse," and
machia, "fighting." (For another mouse word, see MUSCLE.)

BEEF OLIVE

If you've ever eaten a *beef olive*, then you know that it isn't
really an olive at all. Instead, this culinary creation is made from
thick slices of beef rolled with onions and herbs and stewed in a
brown sauce.

To make matters even more confusing, the roots of the expression *beef olive* have nothing to do with bovines and everything to
do with birds. The *olive* in beef olive is an alteration of *alou*, the
Old French word for lark (as in the "little lark," or *alouette*, of children's-song fame). The reason is that once these slices of beef are
cooked and rolled, they look like headless birds.

BEHEMOTH

Pronounced either "bih-HEE-muth," or "BEE-uh-muth," this word, which means "something enormous," originates in the description of a mighty animal mentioned in Hebrew scripture. In the Book of Job, verses (40:15–19) are part of a section designed to demonstrate the might of God:

Behold, Behemoth which I made as I made you; he eats grass like an ox. Behold his strength in his loins, and his power in the muscles of his belly. He makes his tail stiff like a cedar; the sinews of his thighs are knit together. His bones are tubes of bronze, his limbs like bars of iron.

The Hebrew word here, *behemoth,* is an intensive form of a word meaning "beast." Many scholars think the writer specifically used this word to mean "hippopotamus," since elsewhere Behemoth is described as living in marshes or along the river Jordan. Others speculate that this name derives from the Egyptian term *p-ehe-mau,* meaning "water ox." In any case, speakers of English have adopted the name of this hefty beast as a word for anything or any creature that is enormous.

BELLUINE

You don't see this word often, but in the seventeenth and eighteenth centuries, *belluine* was commonly used to mean "pertaining to or characteristic of beasts; brutal." As one writer observed in 1618: "Barbarous cruelty is a belluine quality." Others have used this word when describing *belluine rage* or *belluine life*. It derives from the Latin word *bellua,* meaning "beast," which is also the source of the obsolete word *belue,* which means "sea monster" or "whale."

BELLWETHER

This word's roots go back to the fifteenth century, when *wether* meant "a castrated sheep." Farmers used to fit their leading wether with a bell around the neck, all the better to help the other sheep follow him. This lead wether came to be known as the *bellwether*.

Speakers of English soon applied the term *bellwether* to humans as well, although initially they used it in a derogatory sense, as when referring to the ringleader of a mob. Over time, the word *bellwether* lost its negative connotations, and today we use it in a neutral or even positive sense, denoting a leader or indicator of future trends, such as a *bellwether stock*.

BERNARD

The name *Bernard,* along with its variant *Barnard,* means "bear-strong" or "bear-brave." They derive from the old Germanic elements *berin,* meaning "bear," and *hart,* meaning "strong" or "brave." The etymologically related Swedish name *Bjorn* also means "bear." See BERSERK.

BERSERK

There's a bearskin inside this word: In Old Norse, the term for "wild warrior" was *berserkr*. It's thought to derive from a combination of *bjorn,* which means "bear" (as does the name *Bjorn*), and *serkr,* meaning "shirt" or "coat." (In Scotland today, the related word *sark* still means "shirt.")

Tradition holds that these *berserkers,* or "wild warriors" went, well, berserk—roaring like animals, foaming at the mouth, and even biting the rim of their iron shields. (Some authorities suggest that the warriors' wild behavior may have been inspired at least in part by munching a few hallucinogenic mushrooms beforehand.) In any case, today we use *berserk* more generally to mean "wildly destructive," "frenzied," or otherwise running amok—regardless of what one is wearing, as in "If one more cell phone starts ringing in here, I swear I'll go berserk."

BERTRAM

The name *Bertram,* along with variants *Bart* and *Bert,* was inspired by a "glorious raven." They derive from old Germanic terms *behrt,* meaning "bright," and *hramn,* "raven."

BÊTE NOIRE

The term *bête noire,* which means "a person or thing to be avoided," or "the bane of one's existence," is a French expression that literally means "black beast" (The *bête* in *bête noire* is a cousin of the English word *beast.*)

The expression *bête rouge,* on the other hand, literally means "red beast"—and has been borrowed into English as another name for the red biting mite otherwise known as a "chigger." See BÊTISE.

BÊTISE

We borrowed this word for stupidity or folly directly from French, where *bête* means both "beast" and "fool." It's pronounced bay-TEEZ. (For another beastly French word, see BÊTE NOIRE.)

BEVERLY

The source of the name *Beverly,* as well as its variant *Buffy,* is a combination of the Old English *beofor,* or "beaver," plus *léah,* meaning "meadow."

BIDET

In 1630, the British writer and actor Ben Jonson wrote, "I will return to myself, mount my bidet, in a dance, and curvet upon my curtal." So, was he talking about hopping up on a *bidet* in his bathroom?

Fortunately not. Jonson was using the word *bidet* in its earlier sense, when it meant a "small pony." We borrowed the word *bidet* directly from French, where it also means "pony" or "old nag," and is a relative of the Old French word *bider,* which means "to trot."

By the eighteenth century, the word *bidet* had acquired another meaning in French and English, that of "a low, toiletlike basin popular in Europe for washing one's genitals and back-side." As defined in Francis Grose's 1785 *Dictionary of the Vulgar Tongue,* a bidet (then commonly pronounced "biddy"), was "a kind of tub, contrived for ladies to wash themselves, for which purpose they bestride it like a little French poney, or post horse, called in France *bidets.*"

So Ben Jonson was talking about hopping onto a living, breathing, hay-munching bidet. But what did he mean when he said he planned to "curvet on my curtal"? The expression *to curvet* is an equestrian term denoting the action of raising the forelegs, then kicking the hind legs up before the forelegs reach the ground. This word comes from Latin *curvus*, meaning "curved" or "bent," the same source of the English word *curve*. Etymologists suspect that curvet also inspired our own word *cavort*. In its earliest sense, cavort denoted the action of horses and riders prancing and capering about. In time, the word also came to denote more general frisking about and merrymaking, as in "After a quick trip to the bidet, Vanessa was ready to cavort all over again."

But, you ask, what's a *curtal*? See CURTAIL.

BLATANT

The adjective *blatant* comes from the name of a terrible, blathering beast that had a thousand tongues and a nasty sting to boot. For his 1596 allegorical poem *The Faerie Queen*, Edmund Spenser created a character called the *Blatant Beast*. This vicious monster was the offspring of the three-headed guard dog Cerberus and another fabulous beast, the Chimera. (See CHIMERA.) Spenser created this many-tongued, mythical beast as a symbol for slander, a problem he considered particularly pernicious and pervasive among his contemporaries.

It's unclear what inspired Spenser to call this creation the Blatant Beast. Some scholars believe he may have adapted it from the Latin word *blatīre*, which means to "babble," "chatter," or "prate." It is thought that Spenser pronounced the word *blatant* with a short *a*, although now it is always long. In any case, afterward the expression *blatant beast* remained a synonym for "slander." Meanwhile, the word *blatant* itself acquired the more general sense of "unpleasantly clamorous," "noisy," "loudly bleating," and eventually, "glaringly or offensively conspicuous."

In addition to this term, Spenser's poem contributed yet another familiar word still used today: *braggadocio*. Meaning "empty boastfulness" or "a braggart," this derives from the name of another character, *Braggadochio*, the personification of boastfulness itself. Spenser seems to have concocted this word by taking the English verb *brag*, and giving it a pseudo-Italian ending.

For another mythical beast—this one hidden deep inside your head—see HIPPOCAMPUS.

BOMBASTIC

It would be reasonable to assume that *bombastic* means "loud," "booming," or otherwise "like a bomb." But it would be wrong. Strictly speaking, the word *bombastic* means "empty," "inflated," and "insubstantial." That's because its origins lie curled up inside *bómbyx*, the ancient Greek work for silkworm, the moth larva that spins a silken cocoon used in making the soft, slinky cloth. From this linguistic root arose an Old French word *bombace*, which denotes a type of similarly soft cotton padding. Speakers of English borrowed this word whole and eventually altered it to *bombast*, which originally denoted the "soft down of the cotton plant," but soon proved to be a handy synonym for, as *Random House Webster's Unabridged Dictionary* puts it, "speech too pompous for an occasion," in other words, speech that is overly "padded" and pretentious. (Want another wormy word? See VERMICELLI.)

BOOPIC See BOVINE.

BOUSTROPHEDON

Ever wonder why it is that we read a sentence from left to right, then immediately whip back to the left side of the page before starting the next line? After all, not every system of writing works that way. Some ancient peoples wrote in a pattern known as *boustrophedon,* which used letters that ran right to left, then left to right, then right to left, and so on. Pronounced "boo-stroh-FEE-duhn," the name of this type of writing comes from Greek words that literally mean "ox-turning"—an apt name for lines written in a way that mimicked the pattern of an ox trudging back and forth in a field. Archaeologists have found boustrophedonic (boo-strohf-ih-DON-ik) inscriptions in such places as Crete, Italy, India, Northern Europe, Central America, and Easter Island. See BUCOLIC.

BOUVIER See BUCOLIC.

BOVINE

From the Latin word *bovinus,* meaning "like a cow or an ox," bovine is also used metaphorically to describe someone with characteristics traditionally attributed to such animals—that is, someone who is "sluggish," "dull," "stolid," or "stupid." The term *bovine* belongs to a whole herd of linguistically related bovine words, such as *boustrophedon, beef, bulimia, butter,* and *bugle.* Incidentally, if you want to describe someone whose eyes resemble those of a cow or ox, you can use yet another word from this bovine herd, *boopic*. See **BOUSTROPHEDON**.

BREASTSUMMER See SOMMELIER.

BROCK

The name *Brock* comes from an antiquated English term for the badger, an animal that may be so named because of the distinctive white marking or "badge" on its face. Now used as a dialectal term for "a badger," the English word *brock* comes from an old Celtic name for the animal, which may in turn have its roots in the Greek word *phorkos,* meaning "grey" or "white."

BUCK

The word *buck,* as in "How much do you bet we'll never again be able to buy gas for less than a buck a gallon?" is short for the term *buckskin*. These words date back to the eighteenth century, when the skin of a slaughtered buck, or male deer, was used in North America as a unit of exchange, particularly between Indians and frontiersmen. (For another buckskin-related word, see **QUARRY**.)

Actually, the word *buck* applies to the adult male of several species, whether deer, antelope, rabbit, sheep, or goat. Etymologists have tracked the word *buck* back to the Old English terms *buc,* meaning "male deer," and *bucca,* meaning "he-goat," two words that became indistinguishable after the eleventh century. Several related Dutch words also reflect this former sense, including *springbok*—the name of a small South African gazelle that has a habit of springing into the air when frightened—as well as *reebok,* the Dutch name for a speedy South African antelope.

The latter sense, that of a he-goat, has linguistic relatives in several other languages, such as German, where a goat is sometimes called a *Bock* (which is why you'll often see goats depicted on a bottle of the dark German brew known as *bock beer*). Its Old French counterpart, *boc,* or "goat," led to the word *bouchier*—literally, "someone who kills goats" and by extension, "a dealer in goat flesh." From the French word *bouchier* came our own, more general word for "a dealer in animal flesh"—*butcher*.

Incidentally, there's also the faint image of a male deer—or part of one, anyway—in our phrase *pass the buck*. This phrase originated in the language of poker players. Word historian Craig M. Carver explains it this way in his delightful book, *A History of English in Its Own Words*: "Instead of all players putting up an ante in every hand, the dealer would ante and then pass a *buck,* usually a small article like a knife or a key, to the player on his left. When the hand was over, the player with the buck would ante, then deal the cards, and pass the buck on. Originally the buck was a *buckhorn knife,* a knife that had a handle made from a deer's horn." In other words, when a player passed the buck, he also passed along the obligation to ante up. Thus, in a figurative sense, to *pass the buck* means to hand responsibility off to someone else—which inspired President Harry S Truman to keep a hand-lettered sign on his desk that read THE BUCK STOPS HERE. See **SAWBUCK.**

BUCKAROO

There's a "moo" in *buckaroo*. This slang term for fellow or guy is a corruption of the Spanish word *vaquero*, which means "cowboy" or "cowherd" and comes from the Latin word *vacca*, meaning "cow." (See also **VACCINE**.) Strictly speaking, a *buckaroo* is a cowboy, particularly one whose job it is break untamed horses to the saddle.

BUCOLIC

This word for pastoral or pertaining to an idyllic country life comes from the Greek word for rustic, *boukolikos*; it in turn derives from the Greek word *bous,* meaning "ox," and the stem, *-kolos,* meaning "herdsman." Thus the word *bucolic* is a relative of the French word for cowherd, which doubles as a famous surname, *Bouvier*. (For more words from this herd, see **BOVINE**.)

BUFF

The word *buff* has a multiplicity of meanings: We *buff* a newly waxed floor, we call a NASCAR enthusiast a racing *buff,* we say that someone in enviable physical shape is *buff,* we paint the kitchen blue instead of *buff,* and television interviewers have been known to ask politicians whether they sleep *in the buff*. Strangely enough, all of these buffs arise from the same linguistic source, the obsolete English word *buffe,* meaning "buffalo." Both *buffe* and *buffalo,* in turn, go back to *boubalos,* a much older Greek name for this animal.

In the nineteenth century, when buffalo were still abundant in parts of this country, oil-tanned buffalo hide was a very popular

23

material for making coats and other garments. The dull, whitish yellow or tan color of these *buff-leather* skins inspired the expression *in the buff*—an allusion to the similarity between the color of buff-leather and Caucasian skin tones. Meanwhile, the word *buff* came to be a color name in its own right.

As buffalo skin grew scarcer, the name *buff-leather* came to be applied to other types of soft leather as well. Such materials have proved useful for polishing metal to a high gloss, a discovery which inspired the verb *to buff*.

The notion of polishing to perfection also seems to have inspired the more modern sense of *buff* as an adjective, which we use to describe the impressive results of spending a lot of time at the gym polishing one's appearance.

Finally, professional firefighters in New York City used to wear buffalo-skin coats. Around the turn of the last century, amateur firefighters often volunteered to help out around the firehouses and tagged along to assist in battling blazes. These firefighting enthusiasts emulated the pros in every way possible, right down to wearing buff-colored coats themselves. For this reason, these volunteers came to be known as *buffs*. As a reporter for the *New York Sun* observed in 1903, "The Buffs are men and boys whose love of fires, fire-fighting and firemen is a predominant characteristic." Another noted a few years later, "The buff is a private citizen who is a follower, friend, and devoted admirer of the firemen." It wasn't long, however, before the meaning of this use of the word *buff* expanded to include other kinds of enthusiasts.

BUGLE

The ancient forerunner of today's bugle was made from the horn of a young steer. This instrument therefore went by the

Latin name *buculus,* or literally "young ox." The name *buculus* passed into French and wound up in English as *bugle.* In both these languages, the word *bugle* for centuries referred to "a young bullock," while the term *bugle-horn* described "the musical instrument made from the horn of a young bullock," as well as its brass counterpart. Gradually, the use of *bugle* as the name of an animal gradually went out of fashion, although it was still in use as late as 1881. The musical instrument, no longer needing to be distinguished from the animal, had its own *-horn* lopped off and became simply *bugle.*

BUGLOSS

Although this word might suggest the result of spraying insecticide, *bugloss* is actually the common name for any of several plants, also known as *Anchusa* and *Echium.* The rounded leaves of these plants are distinguished by their rough surface, and therein lies the key to their name. The word *bugloss* stems from a combination of Greek *bous,* or "ox," and *glossa,* meaning "tongue" (a relative of such words as *glossary* and *glossalalia,* or "speaking in tongues").

BULIMIA

This word for an eating disorder characterized by binges comes from the Greek words *bous,* meaning "cow, bull, or ox," and *limia,* which means "hunger." While one might assume that the word would relate to the idea "so hungry I could eat a——," it appears that the *bu-* in this case functions as an intensifier, conveying the idea of "extreme" hunger—that is, a hunger of large (even ox-sized) proportions. See **BUTTER.**

BURRITO

This popular Mexican dish consisting of a tortilla wrapped around a savory filling has a name that literally means "little donkey." This may be because the *burrito* on your plate resembles the rounded back of a donkey, or because it is laden with many ingredients, like a little beast of burden. Speakers of English have been using this food name since at least the 1930s. (For another donkey word, see **EASEL**.)

BUTEONINE

If you want to describe someone as "buzzardlike," the word you want is *buteonine* It can be pronounced "BYOO-tee-oh-nyne" or "byoo-TEE-oh-nyne," and comes from the Latin word *buteo*, "a kind of hawk or falcon," the source also of our own word, *buzzard*.

BUTTER

The ancient Greeks referred to butter as *boútyron*, a combination of the words *bous* and *tȳros*, or literally, "cow cheese." (See also **BUCOLIC**.)

BYRON

The earliest folks named *Byron* most likely tended cows. Byron literally means "at the cow barns" and derives from the same linguistic root as the modern word *byre*, which comes from an old word for hut. The word *byre* is still used in Britain as a term for cow shed.

C

The Roman letter *C* evolved from a Phoenician symbol called the *gimel*, or "camel," as did its similar-looking neighbor, the letter *G*. See **N**.

CAB

In the late eighteenth century, the English borrowed the French word *cabriolet* as the name of a light, two-wheeled carriage drawn by a single horse. The light, bouncy movements of such vehicles inspired their French name: the word *cabriolet* derives ultimately from *caper*, the ancient Romans' name for that prancing, lightfooted farm animal, the goat. (For more goaty words, try **CAPER**.)

English speakers eventually shortened the name for this sprightly, capering carriage from *cabriolet* to *cab*, and began applying it to a wider variety of vehicles. In the late nineteenth century, some entrepreneurs began outfitting cabs for hire with devices to measure the distance traveled and therefore the passenger's fare. Invented in Germany, these devices originally were called *Taxameters,* from the Medieval Latin word *taxa,* meaning "tax," and the Greek word *metron,* or "measure." The French adapted this Latin word as *taximètre.* In English, it became *taximeter,* initially accented on the second syllable, and later on the first. The cabs that used one of these devices to figure passengers' fares came to be known as *taxicabs* (which often live up to their bouncy name, as anyone who's ever taken a cab in Manhattan will attest).

A *cab-horse,* incidentally, was a horse that pulled a cab. These knobby-kneed animals also inspired the picturesque expression *cab-horse knees.* It's one of those you-knew-there-had-to-be-a-word-for-it terms, which, according to slang authority Eric Partridge, means "the effect produced by the wrinkling at the knees of a ballet dancer's tights when on."

CACIOCAVALLO

Because its name literally means "horse cheese," some people assume that the mild, slightly salty Italian cheese called *caciocavallo* comes from mares' milk. (In fact, although tradition holds that this is the case, *caciocavallo* today is usually made from cow's milk.) This cheese is so named because it is molded into gourd-like shapes, then set across a framework of sticks to dry, as if astride a little horse. See CAVALCADE.

CAJOLE

The word *cajole,* meaning "to urge" by wheedling, teasing, flattery, promises, or repeated appeals, apparently derives from the French verb *cajoler,* which means, appropriately enough, "to chatter like a jaybird." (For another "urging" bird word, see KIBITZ.)

CALEB

The name *Caleb* comes from a Hebrew word, *keleb* which means "dog." Some scholars suggest this name honors the canine qualities of affection and faithfulness. Others say it may be a reference to the ancient Calebites' use of the dog as a totemic symbol.

CALLOW

In its earliest sense, the word *callow* meant "bald." For example, in his 1388 version of the Bible, translator John Wyclif used a form of callow to render a passage in Leviticus 13:40: "A man whos heed heeris fleten awei, is *calu* [A man whose head hair has fallen off, is callow]."

So how is it that *callow* acquired its modern connotation of "inexperienced" and "lacking in maturity"—especially since someone who's callow is more likely than others to have a full head of hair?

Here's the connection: By the seventeenth century, speakers of English were applying the word *callow* to very young birds that were still featherless—baby chicks, in other words, that were still "bald." Thus the word *callow* acquired the meaning of "immature."

CALVERT

The name *Calvert* goes back to the Middle English term *calfhirde*—literally, "calf-herdsman."

CAMEROON

Picture the continent of Africa. Along its western shore, just at the point where the Atlantic Coast stops stretching east and west, and instead takes a right turn heading south, there's a bay and a small offshore island. The Portuguese explorer Fernando Poo landed there in 1571 and was so struck by its loveliness that he named the island *Formosa,* which is Portuguese for "beautiful." (For some reason, later travelers decided to honor the European explorer instead, and changed its name to the decidedly less beautiful *Fernando Poo,* which remains its name today.)

In his exploration throughout West Africa, Poo ventured across the bay and up the river that emptied into it. Struck by the the preponderance of prawns there, he named the river *Rio dos Camerões,* or "River of Prawns." That name didn't stick, but the connection between this area and its plentiful prawns eventually resulted in its modern English name, *Cameroon.*

CANAILLE

Pronounced "kuh-NYE" or "kuh-NAYL," this term derives from the Italian word *canaglia,* which literally means a "pack of dogs." *Canaille* found its way into English via French, and today serves as a contemptuous term for "rabble," "riffraff," or "the proletariat." See CHENILLE.

CANARD

We use the term *canard* to mean "an unfounded report," or "absurd story" or "hoax," as in "Don't tell me you fell for that old canard!" We borrowed the word directly from French, in which it means the same thing, but is in its most literal sense, the word for duck.

What in the world is the connection between a duck and a deliberately misleading statement? The French have an idiom, *vendre un canard à moitié,* which means "to make a fool of" or "to swindle." Literally, however, this expression means "to half-sell a duck." It refers to the idea that it's impossible to sell a duck halfway, and anyone gullible enough to agree to such an absurd transaction clearly has been duped.

In the same way, an assertion that is deliberately false is a kind of swindle. Over time the expression shortened to simply *vendre un canard,* and finally *canard.* See DUPE.

CANARY ISLANDS

These islands are named for an animal, but not the one you might think. Around 40 B.C., Juba, a chieftain from Mauritania, then a large area of northwest Africa, set out to explore points west. The Roman naturalist Pliny the Elder left us an account of these journeys, which included a visit to a group of mountainous islands off the African coast. On one island in the archipelago, Juba was struck by the number of large dogs roaming there. For this reason, Juba called this place the "Dog Island," or as Pliny recorded it, *Canaria insula.* (The *insula* or "island" in its name is an etymological relative of the word *insular*—in its most basic sense, "pertaining to islandlike isolation" and *peninsula,* which comes from Latin words that literally mean "almost-island.") The *canaria* in the name of these doggy islands is a linguistic relative of the modern English word *canine.*

It was only years later that the yellow songbirds also found in the region were named.

CANCER

Since antiquity, physicians have observed that malignant tumors often have swollen veins emanating from them that resemble a crab's legs. According to Galen, the second-century Greek anatomist whose theories formed the basis of Western medicine until the Renaissance, the crablike appearance of this sort of tumor prompted the Greeks to call it a *karkinoma,* from the word *karkinos,* meaning "crab." A form of this Greek word for crab found its way into English, via Latin, as *carcinoma.*

The Latin word for crab, on the other hand, is *cancer*—just like the astrological sign of the same name, which is symbolized by the crab. In Latin, the word *cancer* came to mean both "crab" and "malignant disease." The Latin *cancer* eventually gave rise to the English word *canker,* a word which was broadly applied to "any of various types of ulcerations." By 1600, British physicians had begun using the old Latin word *cancer* as an official medical term specifying a malignancy.

CANOPY

Flitting about inside this word for a type of "suspended covering" is the ancient Greek word *kōnōps,* which means "mosquito" or "gnat." The word *kōnōps* led to the word *kōnōpeion,* meaning "a bed or couch surrounded by netting to keep mosquitos away," then later to the Latin word *conopeum,* or "mosquito net," and eventually into the English word *canopy*—"a covering for a bed."

Incidentally, the outlines of this Greek word meaning a "bed or couch surrounded by mosquito netting" are also visible in the French word *canapé,* which means "couch." This French term in turn gave rise to the edible kind of *canapé,* a cracker or thin slice of bread or toast that serves as the "couch" upon which other savories sit.

CAPER

Look closely at the verb *to caper,* which means to "skip about" or "hop playfully," and you'll see a frisky goat doing exactly that. Caper goes back to the Latin *caper,* which means "goat," a relative of such words as the name of the "goat-horned" zodiac sign, *Capricorn.* See also CORNUCOPIA.

Caper is adapted from another another goaty English word, *capriole,* yet another offspring of the Latin word for goat. A *capriole* is "a vertical leap by a trained horse in which it kicks out with its hind legs, then lands again in the same spot." More broadly, a *capriole* is a "playful leap." We borrowed this term from the French, who got it from the Italians' word *capriola,* which means "to leap or caper," and is also from the Latin word for goat.

As a noun, caper later gained the added meaning of "trick" or "prank" or "frivolous escapade," and also "a crime or attempted crime, especially one involving burglary or theft." (This type of caper by the way, has nothing to do with the spicy kind you eat; that type derives its name from the Latin word for the shrub from which it comes, *capparis.*)

Actually, there's a whole herd of goaty words in English. See CAB, CHEVRON, HIRCINE, SCAPEGOAT, TRAGEDY, and TRAGUS.

CAPRICE

The word *caprice* refers to a whim or an impulsive change of mind, or various other types of sudden change, such as "a *caprice* of nature." But to spot its animal roots, one must first know that *caprice* derives from the Italian word *capriccio,* which originally meant "horror."

However, this word inspired by extreme fear is actually quite picturesque: It's a combination of *capo*, meaning "head," and *riccio*, which means "hedgehog." Thus, something shocking or frightening enough to make one's hair stand on end induces what might be aptly described as "hedgehog head."

Over time, the meaning of *capriccio* softened from "horror" to "sudden impulse or whim," possibly influenced by the Italian word *capra*, or "goat," with its connotations of capering and prancing about. Today the Italian word *capriccio* also denotes a freeform musical work characterized by similar whimsy and energy. See **CAPER**.

Incidentally, the *riccio*, or "hedgehog," in *capriccio* comes from the Latin word for the same animal, *ericius*, which is also the source of the English word *urchin*. See **URCHIN**.

CAPRIOLE See CAPER.

CARACOLE

In Spanish, a *caracol* is a snail. Figuratively, this Spanish word also means "a winding staircase." It also came to denote "a half-turn to the left or right executed by a horse and rider"—again, a reference to a snail's distinctive spiral shape. The French borrowed this equestrian term from Spanish, adding an *e* in the process. In time, speakers of English also adopted this "snail" word and likewise applied it to the same equestrian move. See **COCHLEA**.

CARCINOMA See CANCER.

CARMINE See CRIMSON.

CATERPILLAR

Caterpillar most likely comes from an Old French word for "hairy cat," which in turn derives from the Latin words *cattus,* meaning "cat," and *pilosus,* meaning "hairy." (This makes caterpillar a relative of the hair remover called a *depilatory*.)

Strangely enough, this furry little larva has been likened to much bigger animals in other languages as well. In Switzerland, a caterpillar is sometimes called a *Teufelskatz*—or "devil's cat." In parts of Italy, a caterpillar is a *gatta,* or "cat," while in others, it's a *cagnon,* or literally, "dog." The French, on the other hand, call a caterpillar a *chenille*—a word that literally means "little dog." See CHENILLE.

The word *caterpillar*'s final form may have been influenced by the obsolete English word *piller,* which means "robber, plunderer, or thief," and a relative of *pillage.*

Incidentally, if you've used the word *caterpillar* too many times in one paragraph, you can always substitute the word *malshave* (although most people will have no idea what you're talking about). This obsolete word for caterpillar is of unknown origin.

CATERWAUL

The verb *to cauterwaul* means "to howl," or "screech" or "cry like a cat in heat," as in "Now quit that caterwauling and clean out those litter boxes!" The word *caterwaul* can also mean "to quarrel noisily"—to have a catfight, in other words. It derives from a presumed Middle English word *cater,* meaning "tomcat," and *waul,* a word that is probably onomatopoetic and means, according to the *Oxford English Dictionary,* "to utter the loud harsh cry characteristic of cats or of new-born babies."

Incidentally, the German equivalent of this word, *Katzeng'schrei*, or "cats' screaming" is at the heart of the name of a Bavarian dish of boiled meat, onion, and eggs all noisily fried together—presumably making as much of a racket as yowling felines at rutting time. See KATZENJAMMER.

CAVALCADE

Today the word *cavalcade* denotes just about any kind of procession or series, as in "Marvin spent much of his spare time trying to figure out why his love life was best described as one long cavalcade of first-and-last dates." Originally, however, the word *cavalcade* referred specifically to a "ride," "march," or "raid" conducted on horseback. That's because the word comes from the early Italian word *cavalcare,* which means "to ride on horseback," and ultimately derives from the Latin word for horse, *caballus*.

From the same horse-word herd comes the term *cavalry,* which originally meant "military units on horseback." Today this word's meaning has expanded, denoting "highly mobile military units that use motorized vehicular transport, such as light helicopters." Another word from this herd is *cavalier,* which originally meant a "horseman" or "knight," then gradually acquired the meaning of a "courtly gentleman or gallant." In time, the word *cavalier* also acquired the sense of a "boisterous, spirited, swaggering fellow," which seems to have influenced the development of *cavalier* as an adjective that means "haughty," "disdainful," or "offhand in manner."

The French cousin of these words is *cheval,* which likewise produced several "knightly" descendants. One of them is the word *chivalry,* which refers to "the sum of ideal qualities possessed by a knight, such as bravery, gallantry, courtesy, and expertise with weaponry." Another French word that ultimately derives from the Latin word *caballus* is the surname *Chevalier*, literally the French equivalent of the English surname *Knight*. See CHEVAL DE BATAILLE.

CAVALRY See CAVALCADE.

CAVORT See BIDET.

CELANDINE

The name *celandine* (SELL-un-dyne or SELL-un-deen) applies to various types of flowers that have small yellow blossoms. These include the flower that is also called swallowwort—and therein lies the source of its name. The word *celandine* derives from the word *chelidōn,* the ancient Greek name for the bird we call a swallow. According to ancient writers, the connection between the flower and the feathered one is that celandine began blooming when the swallows returned each spring, then withered when they departed.

CERVINE

To describe someone who is deerlike, you can always use the word *cervine*. Pronounced "SURR-vyne," this word derives from the Latin name for the deer, *cervus*. The word also describes anything having a "deep, tawny color," like the coloration of a fawn. (For another expression with a deer in it, see HUMBLE PIE.)

CHAMELEON See DANDELION.

CHATOYANT

The shimmering image inside the exceedingly lovely word *chatoyant* will be familiar to any cat lover. Pronounced "shuh-TOY-unt," this word describes anything "shifting in luster or color, as a cat's eyes do." *Chatoyant* derives from the French verb *chatoyer,* which literally means "to shimmer like cats' eyes." It's a relative of the French word *chat,* which is cognate with our own three-letter term for a feline. See **AILUROPHILE**.

CHENILLE

If you've ever fingered the soft, tufted cords on a *chenille* bedspread, then you'll understand why this fabric takes its name directly from the French word *chenille,* which means "caterpillar." To make matters even more complicated, though, the French name for the furry little creature derives from the Latin word *canicula,* which literally means "little dog." (For more about this linguistic cross-species breeding, see **CATERPILLAR**.)

CHEVAL DE BATTAILLE

Speakers of English borrowed the phrase *cheval de battaille* from French, where it literally means "battle-horse." In both languages, however, it has also come to mean "an obsession" or "a favorite topic of argument or discussion." As in "Oh dear, it looks like Clarence is up on his high horse again, going on and on about his new *cheval de bataille:* the relative merits of pot-bellied pigs and Pomeranians." See CHEVAL-DE-FRISE.

CHEVAL-DE-FRISE

The military term *cheval-de-frise* is another we adopted from French, in which it denotes "an obstacle set up for defensive purposes, consisting of barbed wire or spikes projecting from a wooden frame." Literally, however, this expression means "a horse from Friesland." The phrase arises from the fact that during the latter half of the seventeenth century, the Germanic people known as the Frisians tried to make up for their lack of a cavalry by setting up nasty obstacles to impede the progress of enemy armies.

Since then, the term *cheval-de-frise* has also come to apply to a row of sharp projections attached to the top of a wall, such as spikes or pieces of broken glass, to fend off intruders. In the eighteenth century, the plural, *chevaux-de-frise,* was put to more benign use, referring to "the jagged edges of women's hats and dresses." The writer Washington Irving used a variant of this expression to fine effect when he described someone this way: "When he smiled, there appeared from ear to ear a *chevaux-de-frise* of teeth." See CHEVAL GLASS.

CHEVALET See CHEVAL GLASS.

CHEVALINE See CHEVAL GLASS.

CHEVAL GLASS

The type of full-length mirror known as a cheval glass takes its name from *cheval,* the French word for horse, a term that doubles as a synonym for "a supporting framework." See **EASEL**. In the case of a cheval glass, the mirror is mounted on a supporting frame that allows the mirror to be tilted.

A related word is *chevalet,* which denotes "the bridge supporting the strings of a violin or similar instrument." We borrowed this musical term directly from French, in which *chevalet* is a "little horse." All of these equine words are the linguistic kin of *chevaline,* a fancy term for something that has enjoyed a resurgence in popularity in Europe lately: "horse flesh eaten as food."

CHEVRON

There's a goat in this word for various **V**-shaped things, such as the angled stripe on a sleeve that indicates military rank, a **V**-shaped pattern in architecture, or a type of herringbone weave.

We borrowed the word *chevron* directly from French, in which it also denotes a "rafter" or "circumflex accent," but it is thought to derive ultimately from *caper,* the Latin word for goat. Etymologists suspect that the connection between the angled image and the animal lies either in the **V**-shape of a goat's horns, or the inverted **V**-shape formed by a goat's splayed legs. In any case, the word *chevron* hails from the same flock of "goat" words as *chèvre,* the name of a type of "goat's-milk cheese."

CHÈVRE See CHEVRON.

CHIMERA

In Greek myth, the *Chimera* was a fire-breathing she-monster, who was part lion, part goat, and part serpent. Her name derives from the Greek *chimaira,* which specifies a "she-goat." Pronounced either "kih-MEER-uh" or "kye-MEER-uh," it may be a relative of the English dialectal word *gimmer,* which means "year-old ewe."

Speakers of English borrowed the name of this goaty Greek beast and now apply it more broadly to any imaginary monster of similarly mixed parentage. From the *Chimera*'s name we also get the modern English words *chimeric* and *chimerical,* which apply to anything similarly "unreal," "imaginary," "wildly fanciful," or "highly improbable." (As in "Edgar, how many times do I have to tell you that you can't make a profit running a Web site based on such a chimerical plan?")

You will probably hear a lot more of this word in the years to come. Recently scientists adopted the term *chimera* as a term that denotes "an organism or organ consisting of at least two tissues of differing genetic composition, produced through an organ transplant, a graft, or by genetic engineering." Speaking of hybrid monsters, there's also one trapped inside your head. See HIPPOCAMPUS.)

CHIPPY

The slang term *chippy,* also spelled *chippie,* means a "promiscuous young woman," or more specifically, "a prostitute." It appears that some type of animal inspired this word, although etymologists disagree about exactly which one. Some believe that the word *chippy* is short for *chipping sparrow,* the name of a bird commonly found in urban areas. (This explanation conforms to the way other bird words are applied somewhat disparagingly toward women, such as *bird, chick,* and *hen,* the last of these doubling as a word for "a nosy or fussy old woman.")

According to *The Dictionary of American Slang,* however, the term *chippy* may allude to "the chirping sound of a sparrow, squirrel, or other small creature, suggesting the gay frivolity of such women." Still others suggest that the word *chippy* hatched from the French word *chipie,* which means "shrewish woman" or "vixen." This French term, in turn, is thought to derive from *chipe pie,* another French bird expression meaning "thieving magpie."

Whatever animal it commemorates, the word *chippy* was first recorded in nineteenth-century New Orleans. In fact, jazz great Louis Armstrong, who was born there, used the word memorably in his 1954 autobiography: "I had been brought up around the honky-tonks on Liberty and Perdido where life was just about the same as it was in Storyville except that the chippies were cheaper."

CHIVALRY See CAVALCADE.

CHUBBY

The *chub* is a dusky green river fish with a white belly, notable for its obese appearance. The origin of this fish's name is obscure, but since at least the early seventeenth century, speakers of English have applied the adjective *chubby* to someone who's similarly plump. Hence also the handy adjectives *chub-cheeked, chub-faced,* and *chub-headed.*

COCCAGEE

The *coccagee* is an apple common in Ireland; it's also the name of a cider made from this fruit. The word *coccagee* (pronounced COCK-uh-GHEE), is adapted from the Irish expression *cac a' gheidh,* literally "goose turd," a reference to the greenish yellow color of both. As in "Care for a bite of my coccagee?"

COCCYX

Your *coccyx,* or "tailbone," has a cuckoo in its name. Early anatomists apparently saw a resemblance between this bone's triangular shape and the distinctive beak of the cuckoo bird. The second-century Greek physician Galen called this bone the *kokkyx,* or in Greek, "cuckoobird," and later anatomists Latinized it as *coccyx.* It's pronounced "KOCK-six."

COCHLEA

That spiral-shaped cavity deep inside your ear called the *cochlea* takes its name from the Latinized version of the Greek word *kohklias,* meaning "snail with a spiral shell." See **CARACOLE.**

Incidentally, notable snail words in other languages include the Italian word *chiocciola,* which literally means "snail," but also denotes the @ symbol. In France this sign usually goes by more formal names, but the French sometimes refer to it as an *escargot.* The same occurs in several other languages; the word for snail doubles as a name for the @ sign in Korean, *dalphaengi;* Esperanto, *heliko;* and sometimes in Hebrew, *shablul.* (A more common Hebrew name for this symbol is equally memorable: in Israel, you more often hear the @-sign called a *strudel,* just like the rolled-up dessert. Swedes have a similar idea; they sometimes refer to this sign as a *kanelbulle,* or "cinnamon bun.")

In fact, this symbol's curious shape has inspired a host of animal-related names in other languages. In Hungarian, the @-sign is a *kukac*—literally, a "worm" or "maggot." In Russian, it's a *sobachka,* or "little dog." In Greece, the @ is the *papaki,* or "duckling."

The @'s curly tail puts some people in mind of a monkey: The German word for this symbol is *Klammeraffe,* or "clinging spider monkey." In the Netherlands, it's sometimes called an *apestaartje,* "little monkey's tail." Among Serbian speakers, it's a *majmun,* or "monkey," while Bulgarians call it a *majmunsko a,* meaning "monkey *a,*" or simply *majmunka,* "little monkey." In Taiwan, it sometimes goes by a name that means "little mouse," *hsiao lao shu.*

Others see a feline curled up in the @: Finns call it either a *kissanhäntä,* "cat's tail," or a *miukumauku*—literally, the "meow sign." Norwegians, on the other hand, noticed a resemblance between the @ and a porcine posterior; it's sometimes called a *grisehale,* or "pig's tail."

The Danes, however, see quite a different creature; in Denmark, the @ sometimes goes by the name *snabel a,* or "the letter *a* with an elephant's trunk." Their neighbors the Swedes also use this elephantine image. In fact, the Swedish Language Board has recommended this same term, *snabel a,* as the @'s official name. (Then again, the Swedes are the same ones whose lighthearted word for "cell phone" is *nalle*—literally, a "teddy bear"—an allusion to how cell-phone users cradle these less-than-cuddly devices on their shoulders.)

For some reason, though, the English language seems stuck with the least creative names of all for this newly ubiquitous snail-shaped symbol. Although some speakers of English refer to the @ with such picturesque names as *whirlpool, strudel, rose,* and *cabbage,* what we hear most of the time, alas, is plain old boring *at sign* or *at.*

COCKALORUM

Now here's a word that could and should enjoy wider use: According to the *American Heritage Dictionary,* a *cockalorum* is "a little man with an unduly high opinion of himself." The word applies more generally to "boastful talk" or "a swaggering manner," or, in the words of the *Oxford English Dictionary,* "self-important narration; 'crowing.'"

Etymologists aren't entirely sure of this word's origin, although it appears that *cockalorum* is a bird word of one sort or another. It may derive from the English word *cock,* connoting the idea of a strutting bantam rooster. Or it may come from the obsolete Flemish word *kockeloeren,* an onomatopoetic word that means "to crow." See COXCOMB.

COCKNEY

Although today we use the term *Cockney* to denote "a native of London's East End," this word has rustic roots. The word *Cockney* derives from a Middle English term for "a cock's egg." In Middle English, the term *cokenei,* or "cock's egg," applies to any "malformed egg"—one that is unusually small or yolkless, for example—a joking reference to the impossibility of a rooster actually laying an egg.

Over time, this term for a pitiful little egg came to be applied humorously to "a pampered, coddled child." From there, its meaning eventually expanded to include "a squeamish, effeminate, or affected person," and later to "an urban dweller ignorant of country ways."

Eventually the word *Cockney* settled into its current place in the language, referring specifically to Londoners, who presumably would be less hardy than country folk, and in particular to those born within the sound of the bells of St. Mary-le-Bow, a church in east-central London. The term *cockney* (which is sometimes capitalized, sometimes not) now also denotes the distinctive dialect and accent peculiar to this place, as it is in this vivid passage in a 1985 issue of *Time*: "In the most striking moment, she wheels on her daughter, drops her posh accent and snarls a question in the gutter Cockney she spoke as a girl, revealing a whole lost life in the intonation of a few syllables."

COCKPIT

In its earliest sense, the English word *cockpit* literally referred to the bloody cockfighting pits where humans unleashed roosters upon each other to fight gruesome battles to the death. Later, the word *cockpit* came to apply figuratively to any site where a competition is fought out. (Because so many battles have been fought on its soil, for example, Belgium has been called The "Cockpit of Europe.")

By the eighteenth century, the meaning of the word *cockpit* extended to the part of a naval ship set aside for those wounded in battle. In the twentieth century, World War I pilots began applying the word to the place that served as the center of operations for their own aerial battles. The earliest military pilots dropped hand-held bombs from their cockpits, and fired at enemy aircraft using rifles and revolvers. The bird-inspired name for the part of an airplane from which pilots conducted combat operations was carried over into civilian use, so that now every pilot, domestic or otherwise, flies in the *cockpit*.

CODA

We call the "tail" end, or concluding passage, of a musical composition the *coda,* a term we borrowed from Italian, where the word *coda* literally means "tail." See **COWARD**.

COLUMBINE

Look closely at the *columbine* flower, and you'll see that the inverted blossom resembles a cluster of doves, all cuttering to one another. This image inspired the flower's name, which derives from *columba,* the Latin word for dove. In ancient Rome, the word *columbarium* originally referred to "a set of nesting boxes for doves," and eventually also came to mean "subterranean vaults containing niches for storing created remains." Today columbarium refers to similar vaults for housing the ashes of the dead.

Oh, and *cuttering*? This musical word means both "talking privately" and "cooing like a dove." Although its origin is uncertain, the verb *to cutter* may share a common ancestor with German *kuttern,* "to coo like a dove," as well as Swedish *qvittra,* "to chirp," and *kvitta,* an Old Norse word for "rumor." See **PALOMINO**.

COMEDO

Okay, fair warning: the word *comedo* and the story of how it came to be isn't something you want to read over breakfast. That's because a) the word *comedo* is a fancy term for blackhead, and b) it derives from an ancient word for maggot.

In ancient Rome, *comedo* originally meant "a glutton." The Romans later applied the same word to denote "a maggot," the tiny creature known for the gluttonous way it devours things.

It gets worse: Somewhere along the way, speakers of English noticed a resemblance between the shape of a maggot and the contents of a pustule. So they started applying the name *comedo* to what the *Oxford English Dictionary* oh-so-helpfully defines as: "a small worm-like yellowish black-tipped pasty mass which can in some persons be made, by pressure, to exude from hair follicles." Actually, the dictionary goes on to include this useful explanation from an 1874 medical text: "This collection when squeezed out of the skin, is emitted in a cylindrical form, having the appearance of a small grub or maggot . . . hence it is sometimes called a 'maggot-pimple' or 'whelk.' "

In any case, it's worth keeping these grubby little critters in mind when reading the label on fancy makeup or skin products boasting that they're *non-comedogenic*. All this means is that they won't cause zits. See **MAWKISH**.

CONSTABLE

The term *constable* derives from the Late Latin term *comes stabuli,* or literally, "officer (or count) of the stable." In medieval times, the position of the constable was an extremely important one, horses being an integral part of military operations in those days, not to mention everyday transportation. Thus the *comes stabuli,* or in French, *conestable,* was among the highest-ranking officers in a royal household. In fact, in France the officer holding the title of *Constable* served as commander-in-chief in the absence of a monarch.

English speakers borrowed this idea, using an earlier form of the word *constable* to refer to "the chief officer of a court, household, administration, or military force." By the fourteenth century, they had also adopted the phrase *petty constable* (sometimes called *parish constable*) to denote an officer of the peace in a small jurisdiction who also performed administrative duties. This sense of an "officer of the peace" is preserved in Britain today, where a police officer is commonly called a constable—regardless of whether he or she knows anything about horses. See MARSHAL.

COQUETTE

A *coquette,* the *Oxford English Dictionary* tell us, is "a woman (more or less young), who uses arts to gain the admiration and affection of men, merely for the gratification of vanity or from a desire of conquest, and without any intention of responding to the feelings aroused; a woman who habitually trifles with the affections of men; a flirt."

Ironically, the word *coquette* derives from the name of a male animal, not a female. *Coquette* comes from the French word *coquet*—literally "little rooster or cock." The word is an allusion to what the great dictionary calls "the strutting gait and amorous characteristics of the cock." (Incidentally, the English word *cock* and the French word *coq* may derive from the Latin word *coco,* an imitative word that literally means "a cackling.")

At least as early as the seventeenth century, and on into the next, the noun *coquet* in both English and French denoted either a male or female, provided he or she was guilty of empty, and often narcissistic, flirtatiousness. (In 1728, one writer observed, "The coquets of both sexes are self-lovers, and that is a love no other whatever can dispossess.") Although such behavior clearly continues today, over time the word *coquet* came to be applied almost exclusively to flirtatious females, and eventually acquired the more feminine ending. See COCKALORUM.

CORACOID

This bony projection in your body owes its name to a raven's beak. The *coracoid process* extends forward from the end of the shoulder blade nearest the arm, and serves as a point of attachment for certain muscles in the shoulder and upper arm. The name of this small hooked structure derives from the Greek word *koracoeidēs,* which literally means "ravenlike," because early anatomists noted its resemblance to a raven's beak. Something similar happened with another bony bird word. See COCCYX. Coracoid, incidentally, belongs to a whole linguistic flock of raven words. See CORBEL.

CORBEAU See CORBEL.

CORBEL

The architectural term *corbel* refers to a bracket of wood, stone, metal, or brick, projecting from a wall and usually supporting an arch or cornice. *Corbel* derives from the Old French word *corp*, which means "raven." Etymologists have offered several possibilities to explain the connection between the bird and the building term: It may be an allusion to the way that a corbel juts out like a bird's beak. Or it may reflect the fact that in traditional French architecture, these supports were originally cut slant-wise, making them look more beaklike. In any case, the English word *corbel* and the Old French *corp* were hatched from the Latin word *corvinus*, which means "ravenlike," and is the offspring of Latin *corvus*, or "raven."

The Latin word *corvus* also produced the word *corbie*, a Scottish word for crow or raven, which appears as well in the Anglo-French name *Corbett*. A raven is also visible in the delightful expression *corbie messenger*, a term that means "one who returns late, or does not return at all." As in "Don't you be a little corbie messenger tonight, dear!" This expression alludes to a passage in the biblical story of Noah and the flood, in which Noah sends out a raven and a dove to determine whether his floating menagerie was anywhere near land. The raven never returns. But the dove came back with an olive branch in its beak—a promising sign indeed.

But back to architecture. The term *corbie steps* refers to "projections in the form of steps along the sloping sides of a gable," a style common in Scotland, Northern England, and Europe. Some etymologists maintain that corbie steps is a corruption of *corbel steps,* referring to the resemblance between these steps and a series of corbels. Others argue that corbie steps are so named because they provide a convenient perching place for ravens and other birds. This latter explanation is bolstered by the fact that in German, these same structures are called *Katzentreppe,* or literally, "cat steps." (For still another architectural term that involves perching birds, see TORII.)

One more set of raven words: From the Latin word *corvinus,* or "ravenlike," we get the English word *corvine,* which means "pertaining to or resembling crows." This same Latin root now colors a word adopted into English from Spanish: *corvina,* the name of a type of purplish black fish that is the catch of choice for Peruvian ceviche, and is so named due to the raven-black color of its fins. Via French, we also inherited the linguistically related *corbeau,* a term that describes a type of green cloth that is so dark its color verges on black—a linguistic nod, of course, to the color of a raven.

CORBETT See CORBEL.

CORBIE MESSENGER, CORBIE STEPS See CORBEL.

COREOPSIS

The popular garden flower *coreopsis* has a name that literally means "resembling a bedbug." This name, which comes from ancient Greek, has nothing to do with the flower's yellow-to-brownish plants. Instead, the name *coreopsis* alludes to the fact that this flower's tiny horned seeds look just like little insects with antennae. For this reason, coreopsis sometimes goes by the name *tickseed.*

CORNUCOPIA

The word *cornucopia,* which means "an abundance," comes from the Latin *cornu copiae,* or literally, "horn of plenty." According to ancient Greek myth, the original horn of plenty belonged to a goat. It seems the god Cronus had an odd habit: Shortly after each of his children was born, he ate them. At last, Cronus's wife grew fed up, as it were, and while pregnant with Zeus, she devised a secret plan to save her son. Immediately after Zeus was born, she hid him in a cave, and instead handed over to her husband a stone wrapped in swaddling clothes, which he promptly gulped down. Then she gave her newborn son to a nymph named Almatheia, who raised the baby boy on goat's milk and honey. When one of the goat's horns broke off, Almatheia filled it with fruit and fresh herbs. Ever after, the horn was perpetually replenished with nourishing fare for the future supreme deity.

The *cornu* in the word *cornucopia* is the linguistic kin of many other "horny" words, which include *cornet* (the name of a type of horn); *Capricorn,* the "goat-horned" astrological sign; and the single-horned mythical beast known as a *unicorn.* The *copia* in the word *cornucopia* is an etymological relative of other words indicating "wealth" or "abundance," such as the word *copious,* which means "plentiful."

CORVINE See CORBEL.

COSSET

At least as early as the mid-sixteenth century, the word *cosset* has meant "a pet lamb." From this noun arose the verb *to cosset,* which means to treat someone the way a pet lamb is treated—or, as the *Oxford English Dictionary* puts it, "to fondle, caress, pet, indulge, pamper." As in "I'm afraid that, as Mary's teacher, I simply cannot allow you to keep cosseting your daughter by letting her bring that little lamb of hers to school."

COXCOMB

In the late 1500s, the word *cockscomb* meant "a jester's hat"—a name that alludes to the resemblance between a cock's comb—a rooster's bright fleshy crest—and the silly hat with many points. The spelling of this word changed to *coxcomb,* and its sense naturally expanded to mean "a fool or simpleton." Today we use the word *coxcomb* to refer to, as the *Oxford English Dictionary* aptly notes, "a foolish, conceited, showy person, vain of his accomplishments, appearance or dress; a fop; a superficial pretender to knowledge or accomplishments." In other words, if you call someone a *coxcomb,* you mean that he is a "conceited dandy"—which is sort of like saying he's a cockalorum. See COCKALORUM.

COWARD

A *coward* is someone who is likely to "turn tail"—literally. Coward comes from the Latin word *cauda,* which means "tail." Etymologists suspect that the word has its origins in the image of either a rabbit bounding away in fright, or a spooked animal, such as a dog, with its tail between its legs. See PENCIL.

COWSLIP

You'd be forgiven for assuming that this primrose gets its name from the fact that its blossoms are as soft as a cow's lips. Actually, this word's origins are much more earthy: *cowslip* comes from the Old English words *cu,* or "cow," and *slyppe,* which means "slimy substance." The slimy substance in this case may be slobber, but more likely is cow dung. The connection here is that cowslip often grows in pastures, where you might expect to risk slipping in some slyppe. The "cow-droppings" explanation is bolstered by the fact that one German name for this flower, *Kuh-scheisse,* means exactly that. Incidentally, another variety of primrose is called *oxlip,* a name that again appears to be a reference to what you might have to step through to sniff one.

CRANBERRY

When we think of Thanksgiving, the bird that comes to mind is of course the turkey. But there's also a bird in the name of its tangy accompaniment, *cranberry sauce.* The word *cranberry* derives from the German word *Kraanbere,* which literally means "crane-berry." Some etymologists suggest this alludes to the fact that the slender, curved stems of the cranberries resemble the neck of the leggy bird. A more likely explanation is that these berries thrive in exactly the type of boggy, marshy area frequented by cranes, which is why these fruits are also known as *marsh-berries* and *fen-berries.*

Cranes are visible in at least two other English words. See GERANIUM and PEDIGREE.

CRESTFALLEN

A *crest* is a growth on the top of an animal's head, such as a rooster's comb or a horse's mane. *Crest* comes from the Latin word *crista,* meaning "tuft," "plume," or "crest." In modern anatomical nomenclature, the *crista* remains a term that means "a crest or ridge on top of a bone."

To have a crest that is drooping, then, is to be literally *crestfallen,* as when one sixteenth-century writer observed of a rooster: "O how meager and leane hee lookt, so creast falne, that his combe hung downe to his bill [Oh how meager and lean he looked, so crest-fallen, that his combe hung down to his bill]." This image of a droopy tuft or comb has proven useful for evoking a similarly "dejected," "disheartened," or "dispirited" look in humans.

Crestfallen has also been used to denote an equine illness: a 1725 dictionary defined it as "a Distemper in Horses, when the Part on which the Main grows, which is the upper part thereof, and call'd the Crest, hangs either to one Side or the other, and does not stand upright as it ought to do."

CRIMSON

The name of this vibrant color has dead bugs in it. The kermes (KURR-meez) insect lives in small, evergreen oaks in Southern Europe around the Mediterranean, and in Northern Africa. The pea-shaped bodies of the female kermes, when dried and ground up, yield a deep red dye.

From the Arabic name for kermes, *qirmiz,* comes our own word *crimson,* which denotes a "deep or vivid purplish red." The same Arabic source also may have inspired the color word *carmine,* which denotes "crimson or purplish red." See VERMIL-ION and INGRAIN.

CROTALIFORM

For a succinct way to say that something resembles a rattlesnake, the word you need is *crotaliform.* This zoological term comes from the Greek word *krotalos,* meaning "a type of castanet used in ancient religious ceremonies"—a reference, of course, to this animal's early warning system. Similarly, *crotalin* is an ingredient in snakebite antidotes, which is derived from viper venom.

CROTTIN

Crottin (rhymes with "rotten") is the English name of a pungent goat's-milk cheese that is formed into small disks. We borrowed this term directly from French, where *crottin* literally means "animal dropping." In France, *crottins du diable,* or "devil's droppings," refers to an especially strong cheese.

The word *crottin,* by the way, is a linguistic cousin of the English word, *crottels,* which refers to rabbit droppings. But crottels are not to be confused with *fewmets,* which are deer droppings (although you can also refer to deer droppings as *grattishing*). In fact, our language has a surprising variety of terms for what various animals leave behind—linguistic tracks from a time when it was important for everyday people to be able to distinguish one type of droppings from another. For example, if you're on the hunt for venison, you wouldn't want to confuse fewmets with *spraints* or *swage,* both of which specify otter droppings.

For the record, badger poop is properly referred to as *fiants.* A wild boar leaves *lesses,* and a hawk leaves *metessing.* A goat leaves *trindles* or *treddles*. If you sidestep a pile of *tath*, you're following in the footsteps of either cattle or sheep. Step into *scumbering*, however, and you know that a dog or fox got there first. And if you're gazing down at what the *Oxford English Dictionary* helpfully defines as "the convoluted mass of mould thrown up by an earthworm on the surface of the soil after passing through the worm's body," you're looking at a little pile of *worm-cast*.

CROUPIER

This word for a gambling-casino attendant who collects and pays bets, and assists at gambling tables comes from the French word for "a horse's rump," *croupe*. Pronounced either "KROO-pee-urr" or "kroo-pee-AY," this word originally meant "one who rides behind another on a horse." Later this notion of "sitting behind" came to include the sense of "someone who stands behind a gambler to assist him."

CUCKOLD

Cuckold, a derisive term that refers to the husband of an unfaithful wife, is yet another bird word, this one having to do with the *cuckoo* bird. The female of this species has long had a reputation for being adulterous, and not only because some cuckoos mate with more than one partner. Like the ornithological equivalent of deadbeat parents, cuckoos often lay their eggs in the nests of other birds, and leave them for the other birds to hatch. Thus, for centuries, people have compared an unwitting husband who is being cheated on to the unwitting male birds gamely raising the progeny of another bird.

The cuckoo's randy reputation is preserved in words involving adultery in several languages. The ancient Romans, for example, referred to an adulterer as a *cuculus,* or "cuckoo," and in German, *Kuckuk* can apply to either the adulterer or the partner who has been duped. See DUPE.

In English, though, the word *cuckold* refers specifically to a duped husband, not the female of the species. (In his famous 1755 dictionary, Dr. Samuel Johnson asserted that in days gone by, "it was usual to alarm the husband at the approach of an adulterer by calling out 'Cuckoo,' which by mistake was applied in time to the person warned." Similarly, Shakespeare played on this idea toward the end of *Love's Labor's Lost,* when he wrote: "The cuckoo then on every tree / Mocks married men; for thus sings he, / "Cuckoo; / Cuckoo, Cuckoo"—O word of fear, / Unpleasing to a married ear.")

The English word *cuckold* is thought to come from a word assumed to be of Anglo-Norman origin, *cucuald,* from that language's name for the bird, *cucu.* It in turn derives from this bird's Latin name. See COCCYX.

CULICIFORM

If you need a word for gnat-shaped, look no further than *culiciform.* Pronounced "KYEW-liss-ih-form," this term derives from the Latin word for gnat, *culex.* If you have just squashed a gnat, you can always communicate this fact by confessing that you have just committed *culicide.*

CURRY FAVOR

"Roman de Fauvel" is an early fourteenth-century French poem about a deceitful chestnut-colored horse named Fauvel.

Traditionally, a horse that is chestnut-colored, or fallow, has been a symbol of dishonesty. In German, for example, the expression *den fahlen Hengst reiten* (literally, "to ride the fallow horse") means "to behave underhandedly, or act deceitfully." In English, the related word *favel* is an obsolete word that means either "a fallow-colored horse," or more abstractly, "cunning duplicity."

This idea led to the French phrase *estriller fauvel,* which literally means "to curry, or rub down, the chestnut horse," but metaphorically means "to behave deceitfully or hypocritically" or "to try to advance oneself with insincere flattery." The English adapted this horse-grooming phrase as *to curry favel*. Through folk etymology (in which a word changes over time because of mistaken assumptions about its meaning or origin), the phrase *curry favel* became the more familiar-sounding *curry favor*.

Incidentally, to *curry,* as in "to brush a horse with a currycomb," may derive from a presumed Latin verb *conredare,* which may make it a distant relative of such words as *ready* and *array*. (The French word *Fauvel* and the obsolete English horse-word, *favel,* on the other hand, are the etymological kin of such words as *fallow*—reddish yellow—and *fauve,* which is French for wild beast, but in its most literal sense means "tawny.") See FAUVISM.

By the way, the phrase *curry favor* has nothing to do, etymologically, with curry flavor—the pungent powder that gives a distinctive taste to Indian cuisine. Instead, the spice called *curry* gets its name from a similar sounding word for sauce in the Tamil language spoken in parts of India and Sri Lanka.

CURTAIL

Inside the word *curtail* is the obsolete English term, *curtal,* which means "a horse with a docked tail." *Curtal,* in turn, is a descendant of the Latin word *curtus,* which means "short." It also produced the term *curt* that describes a reply that is short or abrupt.

The equine term *curtal* was adapted from an obsolete French word, *courtault,* which denoted a wide range of things involving the quality or condition of being short—everything from a "short, dumpy man," to a "short piece of artillery" to a "short bassoon," as well as an animal with a shortened tail. Apparently influenced by the word *tail* and the Middle English verb *taillen,* meaning "to cut," the English word *curtail* eventually lengthened into *curtail.* See **BIDET.**

By the late sixteenth century, *curtail* commonly meant "to make into a curtal by docking the tail," as when a 1577 manual on farming said of one animal: "Hys tayle is . . . a great commoditie to him to beate away flies; yet some delight to have them curtailed, specially if they be broade buttockt." Over time this word's meaning expanded beyond the action of lopping off animal tails to that of cutting off or abbreviating just about anything. See **DOCK.**

CYGNEOUS

If you want to describe someone or something as "swanlike," or "curved like a swan's neck"—or if you ever need a rhyme for the word *igneous*—you can always use *cygneous.* This word is a relative of the proper English term for a young swan, *cygnet,* as well as *Cygnus,* the Latin name of the constellation also known as the Northern Cross.

CYNICAL

In ancient Greece, one sect of philosophers fervently believed that the essence of human virtue is self-control. Deeply contemptuous of wealth and pleasure, these philosophers were famous for scorning comfort, eating raw meat, and neglecting both common courtesy and personal hygiene.

Today we refer to this group of philosophers as the *Cynics,* but in ancient Greece they were called the *Kynikoi,* a name that translates as "the doglike ones." It appears that this name was inspired by antics of the group's most famous member, Diogenes of Sinope, whose snarling, unruly behavior earned him the nickname *Kyon,* or "Dog." For starters, he lived in a tub, and was well known in his neighborhood for such less-than-courtly activities as barking, urinating on people's furniture, and engaging in, well, solitary lewd acts on the street. (As if this behavior wasn't remarkable enough, another member of the Cynics, one Peregrinus Proteus, is chiefly remembered for a decidedly cynical act of his own. During the the Olympic Games of A.D. 165, Peregrinus Proteus committed a rather spectacular suicide by diving into the Olympic flame.)

Relentless in their quest for virtue and highly pessimistic about human nature, the Cynics also were known for sneeringly pointing out the flaws of others. By the late sixteenth century, speakers of English were using the term *cynical* to describe anyone with a penchant for doing the same. Over time, the word *cynical* also came to mean "scornful, contemptuous, or pessimistic" in general.

CYNOSURE

Pronounced "SYE-noh-shoor," the English word *cynosure* means "a focus of interest" or "a center of attention," as in "Our new Web site will be a cynosure in cyberspace." The source of the word *cynosure* is an ancient Greek word that means "a dog's tail." But unless you're a Labrador retriever, you might be wondering: What could possibly be the connection between a pooch's posterior and a focus of interest?

The answer lies in the constellation we call the Little Dipper. Picture the part of the Little Dipper that we think of as its "handle"; the Greeks referred to those stars as the *kynosoura*, or "dog's tail." At the tail's tip is the North Star, which has long served as a guide for sailors. So when the Greeks needed a "guiding star" to help them navigate, they looked heavenward to find the dog's tail—the focus of interest in that constellation. The word *kynosaura* and its English offspring, *cynosure*, belong to a whole pack of doggy words, including *canine*. See CANARY ISLANDS.

DANDELION

The name *dandelion* comes from the French expression *dent de lion*—literally, "lion's tooth"—a reference to this weed's jagged leaves. In fact, another traditional name for this plant is *lion's tooth*. (A still more evocative English name for the dandelion is *pissabed*. Like its French counterpart *pissenlit,* this name for the dandelion refers to the fact that its leaves—sometimes collected and eaten as *pissabed salad*—possess what one nineteenth-century medical text describes as "unquestionably diuretic powers.")

Speaking of lions, these regal creatures are on the prowl in several other familiar words. The *chameleon* takes its name from the way the ancient Greeks playfully dubbed this little lizard a "dwarf lion," or *khamaileon*—literally, "a lion on the ground." Then there's the long-haired little dog called a *Shih Tzu*. Long bred in imperial China as a pet for nobility, the *Shih Tzu* takes its name from Chinese words that mean "lion dog."

Finally, the Hindi surname *Singh* literally means "lion," and shares a common ancestor with the name *Singapore,* which derives from the Sanskrit *Singhapura*—a name that literally means "the lion city." See LEO.

DEBORAH

The name *Deborah,* along with its variants *Debra* and *Devora,* derives from the Hebrew word *devorah,* which means "bee." But that's not the only familiar name in English that means "bee." See **MELISSA**.

DELPHINIUM

A "little dolphin" peeks out of the name of this flower. To the ancient Greeks, the nectary or nectar-producing part of this flower, apparently resembled a dolphin's nose. So they called it *delphinion,* the diminutive form of *delphis,* their name for this marine mammal. Today its Latinized form, *delphinium,* serves as this flower's scientific name. To sixteenth-century speakers of English, however, the same pointy structure on this blossom looked more like the spur on the leg of a bird—hence, its other name, *larkspur.* Surprisingly enough, that's not the only English word inspired by a bird's spur. See **ERGOT**.

DESERET ALPHABET

If you've spent any time in Utah, you've probably encountered the word *Deseret.* It's the name of, among other things, a town, a wilderness area, and the state's first newspaper, the *Deseret News.* In fact, the whole state of Utah goes by the nickname *Deseret.*

So just what is a deseret, anyway? This word first appeared in the Book of Mormon, where a *deseret* is a "honeybee." The term appears in a passage describing the westward movement of the Jaredites: "And they did carry with them deseret, which by interpretation, is a honey bee; and thus did they carry with them swarms of bees. . . ."

Early Mormons in what is now Utah adopted this busy insect

as a role model of productivity and industriousness, even naming that area "The Provisional State of Deseret." Congress refused to recognize their state, however, and instead created the Utah territory, named for a local tribe, the Utes. To this day, the Utah state flag features a picture of a beehive, and the state's succinct motto, "Industry," has distinctively apian overtones.

But here's what's really interesting about the word *deseret,* especially if you're a word lover: it's in the name *Deseret Alphabet,* which denotes one the most intriguing attempts ever to reform the English language's haphazard system of spelling. In the mid-nineteenth century, Mormons were already focusing energies on winning foreign converts to their new religion. As part of that effort, Brigham Young, leader of the Latter-Day Saints, championed the idea of a devising a simplified system of spelling to make it easier for foreigners to learn the often confusing English tongue.

At the urging of church leaders, the first British convert to this new faith, George D. Watt, devised a strange-looking alphabet of thirty-eight characters that were supposed to represent all the phonetic sounds in English. Watt himself was known as an expert in the Pitman method of shorthand, and his training probably influenced the look of his squiggly characters. There is also speculation that his invented alphabet reflects his familiarity with Greek letters as well as others found in The *Book of Mormon.*

Wildly enthusiastic about this new method of writing, Young pushed his followers to learn it. As historian David L. Bigler points out in *Forgotten Kingdom: The Mormon Theocracy in the American West, 1847–1896,* the Deseret Alphabet would not only offer the chance to help foreign converts learn English quickly, it would protect secrets from the prying eyes of outsiders, and if Mormon primers and children's books were published with this system, the church could easily control what youngsters were allowed to read.

However, like most attempts to force people to change their linguistic ways, the Mormons' attempt at orthographic reform failed miserably. By 1869, just a few years after its introduction, the Deseret Alphabet fell into disuse. For one thing, printing proved costly, since this alternative alphabet required the manufacture of special type. The Mormons did manage to publish a couple of Deseret schoolbooks, and for a while, these invented letters also appeared on Mormon coins. Still, despite Young's deseret-like industriousness in pushing this new system, his followers gave up and went back to their old way of spelling—and the alphabet that begins with a "bee" became little more than a linguistic curiosity.

DOCK

In the fourteenth century, the word *dock* was a noun meaning "the solid or fleshy part of an animal's tail, such as a horse's." The origins of this word are uncertain, although it's no relation to the type of dock that lies along a waterfront. The animal-tail dock appears to be the etymological kin of *dockr,* the modern Icelandic term for a stumpy tail.

The noun form, *dock,* led to the verb *to dock,* which first meant "to cut short, especially to cut short a tail." Over time, this sense of "to cut short" expanded to include the action of depriving an employee of a portion of his or her pay, especially as punishment. See CURTAIL.

DOG DAYS

What does the hottest, most sultry period of late summer have to do with canines? The origin of this expression lies in the heartwarming story of a giant and his dog. In Greek mythology, a giant named Orion was a mighty hunter who had many harrowing adventures, which included having his eyes poked out by a potential father-in-law, then miraculously having his sight restored by looking directly into the rays of the sun. Like many hunters, Orion had a devoted dog, and when the pup passed on, the gods rewarded him for his years of faithful service by transforming him into a single bright star that could forever roam the heavens with his owner. The Romans nicknamed this star *Canicula,* meaning "little dog" in Latin.

So, you may still be asking, what does the hottest, most sultry period of late summer have to do with dogs? It seems that in late summer, there are several days when the star Canicula rises and sets right along with the sun. For this reason, the Romans surmised that the weather was made even hotter by the "little dog" that tagged along with the sun. So they called those sweltering weeks the *diēs caniculārēs,* or "Dog-Star days"—the forerunner of our own *dog days.*

DOGGEREL

The word *doggerel* denotes verse that is comic, bad, or crude—or all three. As in "While composing a bit of doggerel to read at the boss's retirement party, Jackson leaned back in his chair and tried to think of a rhyme for 'good riddance.' " The word appears to be yet another lexical reflection of the fact that throughout much of human history, dogs have been held in low regard. As one early seventeenth-century writer suggested, "In doggrell Rimes my Lines are writ As for a Dogge I thought it fit." This notion connecting dogs with, as the *Oxford English Dictionary* puts it, anything "bad, spurious, bastard, mongrel" is evident in several other terms. There's *dog Latin,* for example, which, like pig Latin is "jargon meant to look like Latin," and *dog Greek,* as in the following line from a nineteenth-century text: "Agnostic is only dog Greek for 'don't know.' "

DORCAS See TABITHA.

DUPE

Pity that poor hoopoe, a bird long considered stupid. The hoopoe's reputation as a dullard may stem from the fact that this bird doesn't always lay its eggs in a nest; often it's willing to settle for any old niche it happens to find, such as a hole in a wall or tree. (Speaking of which, see NICHE.) Another reason for its goofy image: the bird's head is adorned with an unusual, fanlike crest, which indeed looks a little silly. Finally, the hoopoe, which is found throughout Europe and Africa, eats insects and worms, and quite often goes hunting for them in piles of manure—a habit that might also contribute to its dopey image.

The hoopoe's name derives for the Romans' word for this bird nerd, *upupa,* which was apparently inspired by the sound a hoopoe makes. (This bird's modern scientific name is even more musical: *Upupa epops.*)

The hoopoe's Latin name, *upupa,* wound up in Middle French as *uppe,* where the expression *tête d'uppe,* or "hoopoe head," became a joshing term for a "fool" or "simpleton." From *tête d'uppe,* or "hoopoe head," came the shortened *d'uppe,* the French term that is apparently the source of our own version of this word, *dupe*. As a noun, it refers to someone easily fooled or deceived or an unwitting pawn. As a verb, *dupe* means "to make a fool of." See CANARD.

E

EARMARK

Since at least the early sixteenth century, the term *earmark* literally has meant "a mark made on the ear of an animal, such as a cow or sheep, as a sign of ownership." Its meaning has expanded to include any "distinguishing characteristic" or "identifying mark." Similarly, *to earmark* now means more generally "to mark," or in other words, "to set aside something for a specific purpose." As in "We'd earmarked those funds for the renovation, but this morning's backup in the sewer pipe may change all that."

EASEL

The *easel* that supports a canvas takes its name from the Dutch that means both "ass" (as in donkey) and "easel." The idea here is that the easel, or in Dutch, the *ezel*, carries a load just like a living, breathing beast of burden. A similar idea is expressed in the Italian word for easel, *cavalletto,* which literally means "little horse."

The words *easel, ezel* and *Esel,* the German word for donkey, are all the offspring of the Latin word *asinus,* making them relatives of our adjective that describes anything or anyone comparable to an ass. See ASININE.

EGREGIOUS

Egregious, comes from the Latin word *egregius,* meaning "outstanding" or "preeminent." In its earliest sense, however, egregious meant "towering over the flock"—from the Latin words *ex* meaning "out" and *grex,* "flock." In fact, although today we usually associate the English adjective *egregious* with negative characteristics—an egregious error, for example—the original sense of egregious was quite positive. In the sixteenth century, for example, English speakers used egregious to mean "distinguished," "excellent," "renowned," and "remarkable in a good sense." While modern translations of Exodus 38:23 allude to an artisan named Aholiab and describe him as "a cunning workman [i.e., a skilled one]," a 1609 translation calls him "an egregious artificer." The use of egregious to mean "remarkable in a bad way" apparently arose from an ironic use of its earlier sense. This herd word has since wandered far afield of its original meaning. It now describes anything "glaringly or flagrantly bad." See GREGARIOUS.

EGRI BIKAVER

The *bikaver* in the name of this distinctive Hungarian wine literally means "bull's blood." The *egri* is a form of *Eger,* the name of a major wine center in Hungary. Literally translated, when you are drinking this wine, you're sipping "bull's blood of Eger." The same taurine idea is present in the name of the Spanish red wine *sangre de toro,* which likewise translates as "bull's blood."

ERGOT

The word *ergot* refers to a fungus that attacks cereal grasses, especially rye. The fungus forms a curved mass of hard black material that then replaces many of the host plant's grains. These curved masses resemble a rooster's spur, and it is this image that inspired the name of the fungus and the disease it causes. The word *ergot* is lifted directly from the French word for this anatomical structure on a rooster's leg.

This spur-shaped fungus, incidentally, has quite a chemical kick to it, and is the source of several potent substances, including the lysergic acid used in making the hallucinogenic drug LSD. In fact, eating ergot-infected rye grains can cause *convulsive ergotism,* a condition that produces hallucinations, vertigo, and ringing in the ears, as well as crawling sensations on the skin. See FORMICATION.

A 1976 article in *Scientific American* hypothesized that bread made with ergot-infected rye in late-seventeenth-century Massachusetts may help account for the bizarre goings-on that led to the Salem witch trials. More recently, the eerie television series *The X-Files* featured an episode in which people suffered terrifying hallucinations. It turned out that those who did also sported tattoos made from ink that was laced with powerful ergot alkyloids that spurred them to do strange things.

ESTROGEN

The insect called the *gadfly* is notorious for the way its repeated stings can drive livestock into a frenzy. See GADFLY. The Greeks referred to this pesky insect as an *oistros,* and the ancient philosopher Socrates proudly likened himself to an *oistros* forever stinging the state's backside. Over time, this Greek word also came to connote more generally the idea of a "sting," and later, the "frenzy" that such repeated stings could cause.

The Latinized version of this word, *oestrus,* was later adopted by speakers of English as a term for "something that goads one on"—in other words, "a strong impulse or passion." In 1874, one John Morley described some people as "pricked by the *oestrus* of intellectual responsibility." Another later wrote of John Milton's work habits, "He would not write more verses when the oestrus was not on him."

By the 1890s, *oestrus* was also being used as a scientific term for "a vehement bodily appetite or passion," and specifically to the "recurring state of sexual excitement in most female mammals, just prior to ovulation, during which she is most receptive to mating," according to the *Oxford English Dictionary.* Today we also spell this term *estrus* and refer to the female sex hormone responsible for "generating" *estrus* as *estrogen.*

EVERETT

The name *Everett* conjures the image of someone "strong as a boar." It derives from the Old English words *eofor,* meaning "boar," and *heard,* meaning "strong." See **APRINE**.

EXCORIATE See QUARRY.

FAULKNER

The family name of one of the most famous writers in the English language, *Faulkner,* is a variant of *Falconer,* various versions of these names being applied at least as early as the fourteenth century to anyone who raises, trains, or hunts with falcons.

FAUVISM

Among the adherents of *Fauvism,* a style of painting that flourished from 1898 to 1908, was the French painter Henri Matisse. Painting from nature, these artists made work marked by expressive vigor and pure, brilliant color. Like so many innovative movements in art, this new style was shocking in its day. In fact, the energy and "wildness" of their work prompted the French art critic Louis Vauxcelles to refer to these artists as *fauves,* or literally "wild beasts." The story goes that in 1905, when Vauxcelles was strolling through the first formal exhibition of such work in Paris, he happened upon a statue by the early Renaissance sculptor Donatello and supposedly exclaimed, *"Donatello au milieu des fauves,"* or "Donatello among the wild beasts!" See **CURRY FAVOR**.

FAVEL See CURRY FAVOR.

FAWN

The word *fawn* originally was an animal term, but it had nothing to do with a young deer. According to the *Oxford English Dictionary,* the word's earliest meaning was "to exhibit affection or attempt to please, as a dog does by wagging its tail, whining or cringing."

Although this word was mostly associated with dogs, it extended to a few other animals as well, as in a 1398 text that noted, "A lambe . . . fawnyth wyth hys taylle when he hath founde his moder [A lamb fawns with his tail when he has found his mother]." Shakespeare referred to "Low-crooked curtsies, and base Spaniell fawning." And in his 1675 translation of *The Odyssey,* Thomas Hobbes used the word in its original sense to render the exquisitely touching scene near the end of *The Odyssey* when Odysseus returns home and is recognized only by his faithful dog, Argus, now quite elderly: "The old dog Argus . . . fauned with his tail, but could not rise."

Over time, the verb *fawn* also acquired the more general meaning of "to seek favorable attention by flattery and obsequious behavior." This word that originally applied to a wagging dog is adapted from an Old English word that means "to rejoice," *faegnian.* The Bambi type of fawn is etymologically unrelated to the doggy verb *to fawn*; the fawn that is born to a doe has its linguistic origins in the Latin word *fetus,* or "offspring." See ADULATION.

FEE See PECULIAR.

FEISTY

The origins of the term *feisty* are surprisingly smelly, for inside this word there's a gassy little dog. *Feisty,* which means "high-spirited," "pugnacious," or "spunky," comes from the word *feist,* which denotes "a small, mongrel dog." It is a variant of *fist,* which means "to fart." (It is unrelated to the *fist* of a clenched hand.)

The verb to *fist* occurs in several old epithets for farting dogs, such as *fisting hound* and *fisting cur.* These expressions eventually were shortened to the contemptuous terms *fist* and *feist,* both of which are still used in parts of the United States to denote a "small, mongrel dog, particularly a belligerent or yappy one." As in "Hey, your feist just ran off with my Hush Puppies!" Today the word *feisty* describes someone similarly spirited or touchy—although, mercifully, this adjective has lost its more aromatic connotations.

FERN

The plant name *fern* derives from an extremely ancient root meaning "feather," an allusion to its delicate fronds. Actually, a similar bird word connection occurs in ancient Greek, where the word *pteron* means "wing" or "feather," and a fern is a called *pteris.* See HELICOPTER.

FEWTERER

If you're one of those kind souls who has adopted a retired greyhound, then pat yourself on the back and call yourself a *fewterer*—a term that literally means "a keeper of greyhounds." The word derives from a form of a Gaulish word for greyhound, *vertragus,* which apparently comes from an old Celtic term that means "run very fast," which, of course, greyhounds do.

FIELD TRIAL

Today we usually think of a *field trial* as a test of a product—a new type of drug, for instance—to determine its efficacy and usefulness in real-life situations. In its earliest sense, however, the expression *field trial* denoted a test of young hunting dogs to gauge how well they would do at such tasks as pointing and retrieving. This term apparently entered the language in the mid-nineteenth century.

FLEDGLING

To *fledge,* in its most literal sense, is "to take care of a bird until it is feathered"—that is, to nurture the animal until it is ready to fly. The word *fledge* comes from an old Germanic root meaning "feather," making it a relative of such winged words as *fly* and *flight.* Fledge can also refer to the action of adorning something with plumage, and specifically to fitting an arrow with feathers. Thus *fledgy* is an adjective meaning "feathered" or "feathery," and a *fledgling* is a newly *fledged* young bird. This sense naturally extended to callow, inexperienced humans, as well as anything else "new" or "untried." See **CALLOW.**

FORMICATION

Look again: this word is spelled with an *m*—and means "an abnormal sensation that ants are crawling over one's skin."

The word *formication* comes from the Latin word for ant,

formica, which produced a teeming family of ant words in English. The adjective *formicant,* according to one medical dictionary, describes a pulse that is "extremely small, scarcely perceptible, unequal and communicating a sensation like that of the motion of an ant through a thin texture." *Formic acid* is a colorless, irritating liquid originally obtained from ants; these days formic acid is synthetically manufactured for use in paper and textile dyeing processes, and for making astringents. *Formicarian* describes anything resembling or involving ants, a *formicary* is an "anthill," and *to formicate* means "to swarm with moving beings," as in "Times Square was positively formicating with New Year's Eve revelers."

In case you're wondering, there are no ants—linguistic or otherwise—in a *Formica* kitchen countertop. Formica plastic laminate was invented in 1912 as a type of insulation for electrical wiring. This new material quickly replaced mica, the natural substance that had been used for this purpose. Its inventors called this plastic laminate Formica simply because it was a substitute "for mica." See **MYRMIDON**.

G See C.

GADFLY

A *gadfly* is a "nettlesome critic" or "relentless tormentor," or someone who is otherwise "a nuisance." The word alludes to an irritatingly persistent fly known for having a sting that can goad farm animals into a frenzy. Ralph Waldo Emerson once noted, "The nomads of Africa were constrained to wander by the attacks of the gadfly, which drives the cattle mad." The *gad* in the name of this vexing insect comes from an old Scandinavian word meaning "goad." See **ESTROGEN**.

GALAPAGOS ISLANDS

These famous Pacific islands west of Ecuador are named for the massive tortoises living there. Famed as the site of the 1835 investigations that led Charles Darwin to his theory of natural selection, this archipelago takes its name from the Old Spanish word *galápago*, meaning "tortoise."

GALLIUM

Occupying number 31 on the periodic table, the element known as *gallium* is a rare steel gray to bluish white metal. It was named for the French chemist who discovered it in 1875, Paul Émile Lecoq de Boisbaudran. So, you may reasonably ask, how in the world does anybody get the word *gallium* out of the name *Paul Émile Lecoq de Boisbaudran*?

Well, the answer involves a bit of etymological humor: Because *le coq* in French means "the rooster," the name of the element was formed from the Latin word for rooster, *gallus*. (This Latin word also produced the word *gallinaceous*, which means "resembling domestic fowls," such as the chicken or turkey, and the term *pico de gallo*, a spicy salsa with a flavor as sharp as its name, which in Spanish means "rooster's beak.")

Incidentally, you could say there's one more "rooster" strutting around in the periodic table. Element number 105 sometimes goes by the name *hahnium*, and it's represented by the symbol *Ha*. This substance is so named to honor German chemist Otto Hahn, who won the 1944 Nobel Prize for work on atomic fission. In German, the word *Hahn* means "rooster."

GAMBOL

The verb to *gambol* means to "leap playfully here and there"— to "frolic," "skip," or "caper about"—but it comes from the French word *gambade*, meaning "a horse's jump." See CAPER.

Gambade, in turn, comes from the Old Italian word *gambata*, which in turn derives from the Italian word *gamba*, or "leg." Thus the frolicsome word *gambol* is likely the etymological kin of such leg-related words as *jamb*, the leg of a door, and *gam*, a human leg.

(This variety of *gam*, by the way, is unrelated to the nautical term *gam*, a word of uncertain origin that denotes either "a herd or school of whales," or, as the *Oxford English Dictionary* puts it, "a social gathering of whales at sea.")

GAVIN

The name *Gavin* is the Scots version of the name of the Arthurian hero Sir *Gawain*. These names derive from either the Welsh name *Gwalchmai*, which means "hawk of the plain," or from the Welsh words *gwalch*, for hawk, and *gwyn*, for white.

GERANIUM

Inside the name *geranium* is an image of the leggy bird known as a *crane*. The ancient Greeks called this grallatorial animal a *geranos*. Later they applied the name *geranion* to a type of flower with long, pointed seed pods resembling the bill of one of these birds. The Greek word *geranion* found its way into Latin as *geranium*, and speakers of English borrowed the name whole. Incidentally, another name for geranium is *cranesbill*. See PELARGONIUM.

And the word *grallatorial*? It describes storks, herons, and other wading birds, including cranes. Appropriately enough, this word comes from the Latin word *grallator*, which literally means "one who walks on stilts."

GERRYMANDER

The term *gerrymander* means "to draw the lines of an electoral district so as to give one party an unfair advantage." But this word originated with a political animal—literally.

When Elbridge Gerry was governor of Massachusetts in the early 1800s, his political party engineered the creation of new election districts designed to consign the opposing party's voting power to only a few districts, effectively diluting its influence overall. In doing so, they created one district that had an especially odd shape.

Renowned painter Gilbert Stuart saw a map of the newly drawn district when he stopped to visit a friend at a newspaper office, and was immediately struck by how the district was so irregularly shaped that it looked like some sort of lizard or amphibian. In fact, Stuart couldn't resist drawing a head, claws, and wings to complete the picture. The artist then stepped back to admire his work, so the story goes, and exclaimed, "That will do for a salamander!" The newspaper's editor chimed in with "Gerrymander!" and a new political term was coined.

Today Stuart remains famous for his portraits of George Washington. Gerry racked up an impressive list of accomplishments as well, as a signer of the Declaration of Independence, a delegate to the Continental Congress, and eventually as vice president of the United States under James Madison. Incidentally, Gerry pronounced his name with a hard g, but today gerrymander is most commonly pronounced with an initial j sound.

GOATEE See TRAGUS.

GOBEMOUCHE

Here's another word that deserves wider use. Pronounced (GAWB-moosh), this word denotes "someone gullible enough to believe anything." *Gobemouche* was inspired by the French term *gobe-mouches*—which literally means "swallows flies," and is the French name of the bird known in English as a *flycatcher,* so called because it feeds on insects that it catches in mid flight.

In the same way, a gobemouche is someone so credulous that he'll "swallow anything." Thus the *gobe* in gobemouche is a linguistic relative of the English word *gobbet,* meaning a "chunk or piece, especially of raw flesh." The *mouche,* or "fly," in *gobemouche* is a relative of its Spanish name, *mosca,* and its diminutive, which denotes an even thinner insect, *mosquito.* See MIDGET.

GOBBLEDYGOOK

Congressman Maury Maverick was a plainspoken Texan who found himself exasperated by the stuffy bureaucratic language commonly heard in the nation's capital. In 1944, as chairman of a Congressional committee, he penned an official memo to his colleagues and subordinates, urging them to speak in plain English. "Be short and say what you're talking about," the memo read in part. "Anyone using the words *activation* or *implementation* will be shot."

Maverick condemned such blather as *gobbledygook,* and later said he wasn't sure why that particular word had sprung to mind. "Perhaps I was thinking of the old bearded turkey gobbler back in Texas who was always gobbledy-gobbling and strutting with ludicrous pomposity. At the end of this gobble there was a sort of gook."

Congressman Maverick wasn't the only one in his family to make a lasting contribution to the English language in the form of a word involving animals. His grandfather, Samuel Augustus Maverick, did too. See MAVERICK.

GOSSAMER

There's a goose inside the lovely word *gossamer*, which denotes "something extremely delicate and flimsy." It appears that the word derives from a combination of the words *goose* and *summer*, although the history of the word *gossamer* is itself a bit gossamery, and more than a little complicated.

It goes something like this: The period of late autumn, just before the weather turns consistently cold—the time we often call Indian summer—also happens to be the time when geese are in season. In fact, in German another name for "November" (besides *der November*) is *Gänsemonat*, which literally means "geese-month" and alludes to the fact that this was the month when people traditionally feasted on roast goose.

If you're out for a stroll on a warm autumn day, when the air is still and the sun hits the ground just so, you may detect fine threads of spiders' silk lying across the top of the grass. Etymologists suspect that because these delicate, filmy strands are most often visible during this period associated with "goose summer," they acquired the name we now pronounce *gossamer*.

The German word for gossamer, on the other hand, is *Sommerfäden*, which literally means "summer threads."

GREENHORN

The term *greenhorn*, connoting a "raw, inexperienced person," apparently derives from an older use of *green horn*, meaning an ox with "green" or "young" horns, and therefore not as well trained or useful as its older bovine brethren. The term was first extended to humans during the seventeenth century, when the word *greenhorn* was military slang for a "new, untested recruit."

Today, however, the term applies more generally to someone who is not yet wise in the ways of the world, or otherwise easily duped. See DUPE.

GREGARIOUS

When we call someone *gregarious,* we mean that he or she is highly sociable and known for "delighting in the company of other people." The origins of this word lie in the Latin term *grex,* which means a "flock or herd of animals." This Latin herd word, in turn, produced a whole collection of words involving groups: *aggregate* (from Latin *aggregatus,* meaning "united in a flock"), *congregate* (from *congregare,* "to flock together"), and *segregate* (from *segregare,* literally, "to part from the flock"). See EGREGIOUS.

GRUBBY

The word *grubby* is crawling with bugs. The term *grub* denotes a pale, plump insect larva and derives from an ancient root meaning "to dig" (because that's what it does). In fact, the word *grub* is linguistically related to several other other words that involve digging, including *groove, grave,* and *gravlax,* the last of these being the name of the Scandinavian dish of marinated salmon that originally was cured by burying it in the ground.

Originally, the word *grubby* literally meant "infested with grubs." As happens with so many words, though, this earlier, vivid meaning has faded. The grubs have all but disappeared from this word, and we use grubby more generally to mean "dirty," "grimy," or "slovenly."

HACKNEYED

When we describe something as *hackneyed,* we mean that it is predictable, trite, or worn out from overuse, as in "His stump speech was a long, lumbering procession of hackneyed phrases." It is this last sense of the word, connoting the idea of "worn out," that offers a clue to its equine origin.

The breed of horse called a *Hackney* was developed in England specifically for ordinary everyday riding, as opposed to the stronger, hardier, or faster breeds developed for hunting, hauling heavy loads, or charging into battle. (Some authorities hold that the name *hackney* derives from *Hackney,* a borough of London where such horses were raised. Others suggest that the name of this breed is simply a relative of similar horse names in other European languages.)

In any case, at least as early as the fourteenth century, the word *hackney* referred to this type of everyday horse, commonly hired out for riding, or for pulling carriages sometimes referred to as *hackney-carriages.* Over time, the meaning of the word *hackney* expanded to include anyone who, like the plodding hackney horses, was hired to perform mundane, tedious tasks. In the late sixteenth century, for example, one writer applied the word *hack-*

ney to divine underlings: "Archangels . . . are sent onelie about great and secret matters; and angels are common hacknies about euerie trifle [Archangels are sent only about great and secret matters; and angels are common hackneys about every trifle]."

A shortened form of this sort of hackney—that is, "someone who does menial work for pay"—remains in the noun *hack*, which refers to, as the *Oxford English Dictionary* so depressingly puts it, "a literary drudge, who hires himself out to do any and every kind of literary work; hence, a poor writer, a mere scribbler." Today the word *hack* also applies to cabdrivers who, like hackney drivers of yore, are hired to transport people.

By the eighteenth century, speakers of English were using *hackneyed* to describe anything that, like a poor hackney horse trudging along the same routes every day, was likewise "exhausted" and "overused"—and therefore "commonplace" and "trite." See JADED.

HAGGARD

We use the term *haggard* to describe the appearance of someone who seems gaunt, exhausted, or otherwise "wild-looking." Originally, though, haggard was specific to falconry, referring to "an adult hawk captured for training." Unlike a hawk raised in captivity, a hawk that is haggard is considered wild and intractable, and often has ragged-looking feathers.

The use of the word *haggard* was later extended to humans as well, initially as a way of describing a "wild" look in someone's eyes, as when Charlotte Brontë once described someone as "thin, haggard, and hollow-eyed; like a sitter up at night." Today we also use haggard to describe anyone gaunt, half-starved, or otherwise "ragged-looking from exhaustion, worry, or fright."

HALCYON

The adjective *halcyon* means "calm," "serene," and "peaceful," but at its heart is a bittersweet story about birds. Pronounced "HAL-see-un," this word doubles as the name of the brilliant crested bird also called a kingfisher. Both senses of this word are connected by the fact that the term *halcyon* honors the ancient Greek goddess, Alcyone.

Daughter of Aeolus, god of the winds, Alcyone had married a mortal named Ceyx. In some versions of the story, their marriage was so blissfully happy that the pair dared to compare themselves to Zeus and Hera. Such hubris, of course, didn't go over well with Zeus, who sent a storm to wreck a ship in which Ceyx was traveling to consult an oracle. Alcyone, who had pleaded to accompany her husband on his journey, learned of his death in a dream, and when she went down to the sea to grieve, the body of her beloved washed up on shore. So despondent was Alcyone that the gods took pity on her and changed them both into kingfishers, birds whose devotion to each other is legendary. The Greeks named this bird the *halkyon* in honor of Alcyone.

Tradition holds that just before and after the winter solstice, this devoted pair of birds and their descendants charm the seas for two weeks, making the surface so calm that they can nest upon the waters and hatch their eggs. The modern English phrase *halcyon days* now refers to any "time of happy tranquility."

HALO

Inside the word *halo* there's a pair of oxen trudging round and round, grinding grain for all eternity. In ancient mills, oxen were tethered to a pole attached to a vertical axis, then forced to tread in a circle, stamping grain as they went. The Greeks applied the word *halōs* to this threshing floor, as well as to the circular path worn into it by the animals' hooves.

Over time, the name *halōs* also came to denote other things similarly round in shape—the sun, the moon, or a shield, for example. By the mid-sixteenth century, a form of this word found its way into English. Today, its bovine origins are all but worn away; when we use the word *halo,* we most often think of its abstract application as "a luminous ring around or above the head of an angel or someone saintly."

HANDS DOWN

This expression meaning "unconditionally," or "easily," as in "He won the contest *hands down,*" comes from the world of horse racing. A "hands-down" victory occurs when a jockey's win is so assured that he drops his hands and relaxes his grip on the reins when nearing the finish line.

HANGDOG

Most of us use the word *hangdog* without ever realizing that preserved inside this term is yet another example of humans' long and shameful history of cruelty to animals. As William and Mary Morris note in their *Morris Dictionary of Word and Phrase Origins,* from antiquity through medieval times, dogs and other animals were sometimes convicted of crimes and sentenced to death by hanging. One report from England in 1595 notes that a dog was so executed "for inflicting a fatal injury on a child's finger." Shakespeare himself makes references to this practice in several of his plays.

Today hangdog means "sad," "shamefaced," "browbeaten," or "intimidated"—an allusion either to the look on a doomed dog's face or to the characteristics associated with someone so base or despicable as to be either a dog's executioner or hanged like a dog himself.

HARASS

The word *harass* means "to torment," or "to irritate persistently." In other words, it means "to hound" someone—a sense that is particularly appropriate, since the word *harass* apparently derives from an Old French hunting term, *harer,* which means "to set a dog after." It came from *hare,* a term for the cry used to urge dogs on.

Incidentally, according to the *American Heritage Dictionary, Fourth Edition,* usage authorities are about evenly divided on whether to stress the first or second syllable of *harass.* So, regardless of which way you pronounce this word, no one has the right to hound you about it, much less harass you.

HARRIDAN

The *Oxford English Dictionary* defines *harridan* as a "haggard old woman; a vixen; 'a decayed strumpet' . . . usually a term of vituperation." See VIXEN.

First recorded around 1700, this term for a "vicious, scolding woman" may be an alteration of the French word *haridelle,* which means both "a thin, worn-out horse" and "a large gaunt woman." See JADE.

HEARSE

The word *hearse* has come a long way since its origins in an ancient language of Southern Italy. It derives from the Oscan term *hirpus,* which means "wolf." *Hirpus* led to the Latin word *hirpex,* the name of a type of triangular harrow that was used for tilling the soil—the name being an allusion to the sharp teeth of the tool, similar to those of a ferocious wolf.

In Medieval Latin this term for a harrow became *hercia,* and in Old French, a *herce.* The same name came to be applied to a triangular frame used in church services for holding candles, since the overall shape was the same and the candle holders also resembled teeth. Speakers of Middle English borrowed this word as *hers,* and over time, this name migrated to a similar and more complicated framework for holding candles over a coffin; then to the bier, or platform for holding the coffin itself; and eventually, to the vehicle that transported the coffin.

The wolf that inspired the word *hearse* is also faintly visible in our word *rehearse.* Literally, to *rehearse* is to "re-harrow," or "to go over again with a harrow."

HELICOPTER

The Greek word for wing, *pteron,* whirs inside the name of this "helical-winged" flying machine. Thus helicopter is the etymological kin of that prehistoric "wing-fingered" creature, the *pterodactyl,* as well as the *apteryx,* a New Zealand bird that cannot fly. Also called the *kiwi,* this flightless bird's Greek name, *apteryx,* literally means "without a wing."

HECATOMB

A *hecatomb* (pronounced either "HEK-uh-tohm" or "HEK-uh-toom") is a "large-scale slaughter," as in "the hecatomb that was World War II."

In its earliest sense, however, this word was used in reference to the religious practices of the ancient Greeks and Romans. In ancient Greece, a *hecatómbē* denoted a sacrifice to the gods involving the ritual killing of one hundred cattle or oxen. This word in turn derives from the Greek name for one hundred, *hekaton,* and the word for ox, *bous.* See **BOVINE**.

This bovine word's English descendant, *hecatomb,* has been used to denote any kind of large-scale ritual sacrifice, whether human or animal. The word *hecatomb* has taken on figurative applications as well. An early eighteenth-century writer referred ominously to "hecatombs of reputations," and in his 1820 lyric drama *Prometheus Unbound,* the poet Percy Shelley wrote of "hecatombs of broken hearts."

HENCHMAN

The *hench* in the word *henchman* derives from the Old English word *hengest,* which means "stallion," as does its modern German counterpart, *Hengst.* Although the history of the word *henchman* isn't entirely clear, it seems that in its earliest sense, this term meant either a "groom" for one's horses, or "a squire or other honored subordinate of a royal or esteemed person, who walked or rode alongside that person in processions." Over time, the word acquired its more general sense of "a trusted subordinate," or in a more sinister sense, "an unscrupulous follower, especially of a political figure or cause," or "a lackey, especially within a criminal gang."

HERSCHEL

The name *Herschel*, along with its variants *Hirsch*, *Hersh*, and *Hirsh*, derives from the Yiddish word for deer.

HIPPEASTRUM See PHILIP.

HIPPOCAMPUS

In Greek mythology, the *hippokampos* was a chimerical beast with the forelegs of a horse and the tail of a dolphin or fish. See CHIMERA. Often depicted pulling the car of Poseidon or other sea deities, the *hippocampus* takes its name from *hippos*, the Greek word for horse, and *kampos*, meaning "sea monster." *Hippocampus*, the Latinized version of the name for this mythical "sea horse," now serves as the name of the scientific genus to which seahorses belong. In addition, the modern medical term *hippocampus* denotes [each of two] ridges inside the human brain—ridges that, when viewed from a certain angle, do look something like seahorses. (For more horsey words, see PHILIP. For more monster words, see SNOLLYGOSTER.)

HIPPOPOTAMUS See PHILIP.

HIRCINE

Pronounce it "HURR-syne" or "HURR-sin," but any way you say it, the handy word *hircine* derives from the Latin word *hircus,* or "goat," and does double duty describing anything that either resembles a goat or has a distinctively "goaty" smell.

Because goats have a randy reputation, *hircine* also describes anyone who is similarly lustful or libidinous, as in "Although Vanessa had high hopes for her most recent blind date, he was best described as hircine, and alas, in more ways than one." See TRAGEDY.

HOBBY

In the fourteenth century, the name *hobby* applied to a type of small horse bred in Ireland. Around the turn of the fifteenth century, for example, one English text mentioned, "An Iyrysch man, Uppone his hoby [An Irish man, upon his hobby]." The term *hobby* led to the expression *hobby-horse,* which by the sixteenth century had come to mean, among other things, a toy consisting of a likeness of a horse's head at the end of a stick, which a child could straddle and then use to go galloping about. Later, the word *hobbyhorse,* and its shortened form, *hobby,* would also come to mean "the carved horse on a merry-go-round" or "a rocking-horse in a child's nursery."

By the nineteenth century, English speakers sometimes alluded to the carefree joy of riding such toy horses when describing the playful pastimes they now enjoyed as adults. In 1823 a writer spoke of "The pleasure of being allowed to ride one's hobby in peace and quiet," while another in 1857 said of someone, "He's on one of his pet hobbies." Today when we say someone is *riding a hobbyhorse* or *pursuing a hobby,* we mean that he is embracing a "pet" idea or activity—presumably displaying the same unself-conscious and wholehearted enthusiasm he did when playing with toys as a child.

HOBSON'S CHOICE

When we speak of *Hobson's choice,* we mean a situation in which someone ostensibly is free to choose among several things, but actually has no choice at all. In other words, the person must accept the choice offered, or end up with nothing. A famous example is the declaration attributed to automobile maker Henry Ford, who supposedly promised that his Model T would be available "in any color, so long as it's black."

At any rate, the original Hobson's choice involved a "choice" of horses. The story goes that in early seventeenth-century England, one Thomas Hobson ran a livery stable near Cambridge University, and for fifty years, Old Man Hobson leased his horses to students there. He was especially protective of his animals, and rented them out on a strict rotating system: the most recently ridden horses were kept to the rear of the stable, while the more rested were kept near the front. That way, only the freshest horse of all was available for hire. Therefore a would-be rider would be allowed to rent that horse, or none at all.

Hobson and his take-it-or-leave-it rule must have made quite an impression, for after his death, he was eulogized by none other than the great English poet John Milton. And more than 370 years later, the old horseman's name remains a part of our language in the expression *Hobson's choice*.

HOOCH

A close look at the etymological history of the word *hooch* reveals the faint tracks of a bear. During the 1800s, U.S. soldiers occupying Alaska often took the edge off those frigid nights by quaffing a homebrew they called *hooch*. As one writer observed during the Alaskan gold rush, "Whenever whisky runs short the Yukoner falls back on a villainous decoction . . . known as *hootchinoo,* or *hootch.*" Brewed with whatever was at hand—including molasses, berries, and graham flour—this beverage was most definitely better gulped than savored. (As one writer noted in a late-nineteenth-century history of the region: "The manufacture of hooch, which is undertaken by the saloon-keepers themselves, is weirdly horrible.")

U.S. soldiers purchased their *hooch* from the Tlingit people in a southeastern Alaskan village on what is now Admiralty Island. The newcomers called this town *Hoochinoo,* an adaptation of its Tlingit name, *Hutsnuwu,* which comes from indigenous words that mean "brown bear fort." At first, speakers of English applied their name for this town to the powerful drink brewed there, and eventually they shortened the name *hoochinoo* to *hooch*.

In time, the word *hooch* came to be a more general term for any type of booze, especially the less palatable versions. The name has also been applied to another mind-altering drug, marijuana. (Incidentally, the sippable and smokable types of *hooch* are etymologically unrelated to the *hooch* that denotes a "temporary dwelling" or "thatched roof hut"; the latter gets its name the Japanese word *uchi,* meaning "house.")

HUMBLE PIE

Having to *eat humble pie* means being forced "to humbly acknowledge a mistake." In its most literal sense, however, this expression is about eating freshly killed deer innards. The *humble* in the expression *humble pie* is adapted from an earlier English word, *numbles,* another name for the edible internal organs, such as the liver, heart, and intestines of a slaughtered animal, usually deer. While medieval lords dined on venison, lesser folk often had to settle for pies made of numbles.

By the seventeenth century, the phrase *a numble pie* had given way to *an umble pie*, an expression no doubt influenced by this dish's inferior status. Over the next few decades, as people acquired more urbane tastes, the thought of eating numbles seemed increasingly humble—so much so that in 1664, the famous diarist Samuel Pepys grumbled about umbles in one of his daily entries, griping that a recent host "did not give us the meanest dinner, (of beef, shoulder and umbles of venison)." Nearly two hundred years later, James Russell Lowell articulated the anti-umbles position even more firmly when he observed, "Disguise it as you will, flavor it as you will, call it what you will, umble-pie is umble-pie, and nothing else." See LOWELL.

Today, whether you're speaking literally or figuratively, the prospect of eating humble pie remains unappealing, no matter how you slice it. See QUARRY.

HYENA See LOBSTER.

I

ICHTHYIC

Besides being a swell word to keep in mind for your next game of Hangman, the term *ichthyic* is an adjective that means "pertaining to or characteristic of fishes." Pronounced "ICK-thee-ick," this word derives from *ichthýs,* the Greek word for fish, and is a relative of the English word for the study of fish, *ichthyology.*

For early Christians, the fish served as the secret symbol of their faith, in part because the Greek word for this animal served as an acronym. The word *ichthys,* they decided, stood for *I(ēsous) Ch(ristos) Th(eou) Ý(ios) S(ōtēr)*—which is Greek for "Jesus Christ, Son of God, Savior." Those initial letters still appear inside some stylized versions of the Christian fish symbol today.

By the way, if you get tired of telling waiters that you're an *ichthyophagist* (a fish eater), you can always try a different tack and say you're *piscivorous* (pih-SIHV-urr-uss). A derivative of the Latin word for fish, the term *piscivorous* means "fish eating." See PISCINE.

IMPECUNIOUS See PECULIAR.

INGRAINED

The word *ingrained* is deeply stained with an image of a tiny insect called the kermes, the dried bodies of which were, in ancient times, ground up to yield the deep red dye called crimson. See **CRIMSON**

Ancient Roman writers sometimes applied their word *granum*, or "grain," to these insects, because of the way they resembled tiny seeds. This name found its way into Old French as *graine*, and in fact the inhabitants of fourteenth-century England sometimes referred to such an insect as a *grain*.

Therefore, in those days to *engrain* something was to dye it with that particular type of *grain*—that is, to dye it a deep red color. Over time, the meaning of the word *engrain* expanded to denote dyeing with any color, not just crimson.

Eventually English speakers began to associate the word *engrain* with the *grain* in wood or cloth—that is, with its very deepest structure—and over time, the notion of something *engrained* came to be associated with a characteristic that's fixed indelibly or deep-rooted. By the eighteenth century, the word *engrained* was also being spelled *ingrained*.

JADED

When we describe someone as *jaded,* we mean that he or she is "worn-out and world-weary" or "cynically or pretentiously unfeeling." So what, you might ask, does all this have to do with the beautiful green stone? Nothing, actually. Jade in the sense of "worn out" arose from an entirely different source: an old word *jade* meaning "a worn-out horse." No one's sure how this particular jade found its way into English, although it may come from an Old Norse term for "mare." In any case, the transitive verb *to jade*—that is, "to exhaust by driving hard"—originally applied to horses, but soon applied to people as well. See **TACKY**. See **HACKENEYED**.

Actually, the story behind the jade stone is pretty fascinating itself. Spaniards who chanced upon this mineral in Mexico and Peru in the sixteenth century believed it had the power to cure kidney problems. For this reason, they called it by the name *piedra de ijada,* which means "loin stone" or "flank stone." The French shortened this name to *l'ejade,* and later *le jade,* which eventually found its way into English as plain old *jade.*

JAEL

The feminine name *Jael* comes from the Hebrew word for mountain goat. There are a couple of versions of her story in Hebrew scripture, but the basic idea is that Jael makes a name for herself by hospitably inviting a Canaanite army commander into her tent for supper, then less-than-hospitably does away with him by driving a tent peg through his skull. The name *Jael* is sometimes spelled *Yael*. (For another four-footed feminine name from Hebrew, see RACHEL.)

JAYWALK

The bird called a *jay* has a reputation for several annoying characteristics, such as its ornery aggressiveness and noisy, irritating chatter. So it's hardly surprising that as early as the sixteenth century, humans began applying the term *jay* to people who were similarly annoying, either because they were stupid or garrulous or absurdly dressed. The term *jay* also came to be applied pejoratively to someone considered a rube or hick or bumpkin—a sense reinforced, of course, by the fact that such a person would live in rustic areas where jays are common.

When the term *jaywalk* came into use during the 1880s, it presumably referred to the action of such jays—the unsophisticated folk, who, because they were unfamiliar with city ways, would cross the street where they shouldn't. As an article in the London *Times* noted in 1937, "In many streets like Oxford Street, for instance, the jaywalker wanders complacently in the very middle of the roadway as if it were a country lane."

Incidentally, a bird word may also be the source of another

word for a rustic or bumpkin. According to some authorities, the word *yokel* may be a figurative use of the dialectal word *yokel,* a name applied in parts of Britain to the green woodpecker. Then again, another bird word pokes fun at city slickers. See **COCKNEY**.

JEMIMA

The name *Jemima* comes from a Hebrew word that means "little dove." In Hebrew scripture, *Jemima* was the first of Job's three daughters. See **JONAH**.

JINX

The bird called a *wryneck* is known for the eerie way that it twists its head, writhes its long neck, and hisses when disturbed. (For this reason, it's also called a *snakebird*.) This relative of the woodpecker also has a strident cry, which it makes only during migration; otherwise, it remains strangely silent.

The wryneck's unusual characteristics apparently made it a favorite among practitioners of witchcraft, and in antiquity its feathers were used in magic potions. The Greeks' word for the bird was *iynx,* a word that also came to mean "a charm." By the seventeenth century, this word's English offspring, spelled *jynx, jyng,* or *yunx,* were used to denote either the bird or a magic spell. Etymologists are puzzled as to why the word *jinx,* specifically in the sense of "someone or something that brings bad luck," didn't appear in print until the early twentieth century. Nonetheless, they suspect that the bird and the word are connected.

JONAH

The name *Jonah* is yet another Hebrew word inspired by an animal. It derives from the Hebrew word *yonah,* which means "dove" or "pigeon." The name *Yonah* is often bestowed on both boys and girls born on Yom Kippur, the Day of Atonement. See JEMIMA.

JUMENTOUS

Need to describe something that is "similar to horse urine"? The word you want is *jumentous*. As in "Why, um, Stephen, your first batch of homebrew is, well, . . . quite jumentous indeed!"

The helpful term *jumentous* derives from the obsolete English word *jument,* which means "beast of burden." It appears in early translations of Hebrew scripture. Modern versions, for example, translate Genesis 1:25 this way; "And God made the beast of the earth after his kind, and cattle after their kind, and every thing that creepeth on the earth." A translation from 1382, however, renders this passage thus: "And God made beestis of the erthe aftir their special kyndes, jumentis, and al the crepynge thing. [And God made beasts of the earth after their special kinds, juments, and all the creeping thing.]"

In modern French, a *jument* is a mare. The English words *jument* and *jumentous* have their roots in the Latin word *jumentum,* which literally means a "yoke-beast," and derives from the Latin word *jungere,* "to join." (Thus jumentous is linguistically connected to the words *join, conjugal,* and *jugular,* the last of which comes from the Latin word for collarbone, *iugulum—*

literally, a "little yoke.") The prehistoric root of all these "joining" words also gave rise, via Sanskrit, to the Hindi word for the discipline that aims to create a "union" between the human and the divine, *yoga*.

KATZENJAMMER

The word *katzenjammer* sounds almost as grating as its meaning: "unpleasantness or distress" or a "noisy uproar." It's also commonly used as a synonym for hangover.

But the strident word *katzenjammer* is more evocative still when you realize that it comes directly from German, where *Katzenjammer* literally means "cats wailing." (Then again, having a hangover in Germany may be preferable to having one in Norway. There if you have a hangover, you have *toemmermenn*—or literally, "lumberjacks," presumably plying their trade bright and early inside your head.)

The howling, or *jammer,* in *katzenjammer* is an etymological relative of the English word *yammer,* which likewise evokes the idea of loud complaining. See CATERWAUL.

KHARTOUM

The largest city and capital of Sudan in northeastern Africa, *Khartoum,* lies at the confluence of the Blue Nile and White Nile Rivers. Its name derives from *Al-Khurtum,* an Arabic word for elephant, and supposedly alludes to the fact that the contour of the city somewhat resembles that of an elephant's trunk.

KHRUSHCHEV

In the Russian language, the word *khrushch* denotes the large, loud beetle that English speakers call a *cockchafer,* from the English word *chafer,* meaning "beetle." (Also known in English as a *May-bug,* this insect is very destructive to plants.) In any case, the name *Khruhschev,* the name of the premier of the former Soviet Republic during the late 1950s and early 1960s, derives from the name of this insect.

KIBITZ

If you know the origin of the word *kibitz,* you can't help but see a little bird hopping around inside of it. This handy Yiddishism means "to look on and offer unsolicited, meddlesome advice" or "to chat or make wisecracks (especially when others are trying to work or have a serious conversation)."

Kibitz derives from the German verb *kiebitzen,* which means "to look on while other people are playing cards, especially in a way that's annoying." The word for this activity, in turn, comes from the German word *Kiebitz,* the name of a little bird with a reputation for being noisily inquisitive.

KITE

The high-flying toy that flutters at the end of a string gets its name from the hawklike birds also called *kites* known for their soaring, gliding flight. This bird name arose from the Old English name for such a bird, *cÿta,* which is also a relative of the German word for owl, *Kauz.*

KNACKERED

The British expression *knackered* commonly means "worn out" or "exhausted," as in "Why, Barb, I'd absolutely love to stay and help out with the drywalling, but I'm afraid I'm just *knackered.*" As the *Oxford English Dictionary* points out, in Britain a *knacker* is "one whose trade it is to buy worn-out, diseased, or useless horses, and slaughter them for their hides and hoofs, and for making dog's-meat, etc.; a horse-slaughterer." The verb to *knacker* itself is of obscure origin, and its original sense of "to kill" has been diluted to mean simply "exhaust" or "wear out." For this reason, etymologists suspect that like the English words *jaded, tacky, hackneyed,* and *harridan,* the term *knackered* may be yet another English word that derives from the image of an old, broken-down horse. (See TACKY and HACKNEYED.)

Some authorities, however, note the possibilty of a different explanation, pointing out that *knackers* is slang for testicles. The word *knackered,* they suggest, may simply mean "castrated."

KOSOVO

Roughly translated, the name *Kosovo* means "land of blackbirds," the word *kos* being a Serbian term for blackbird. In Kosovo, a place called "The Field of Blackbirds" is the site of a famous battle between Serbian and Muslim forces in 1389. See MERLOT.

L

LARKSPUR See DELPHINIUM.

LAVI

The name *Lavi* is Hebrew for lion. This regal animal has inspired quite a few names, feminine and masculine. See **LEO**.

LEAH See RACHEL.

LEO

The names *Leo, Leon, Leona,* and *Leontyne* are *leonine* words, in that they are the offspring of words for lion in either Latin *(Leō)* or Greek *(Leōn)*. The masculine name *Leander* and its feminine counterpart, *Leandra,* also belong to this linguistic pride, born of the Greek word for lion, and a form of the Greek word for man, *andros.* Similarly, the names *Leonard* and *Leonardo* derive from an Old High German name that means "strong as a lion." And *Lionel?* He's a "little lion." See **DANDELION**.

LEVIATHAN

Leviathan appears in Hebrew scripture as the name of a terrible writhing sea monster, the slaying of which represents part of God's effort to bring order out of chaos. The book of Isaiah (27:1) describes it this way: "In that day the Lord with his great and strong sword shall punish leviathan the piercing serpent, even leviathan that crooked serpent; and he shall slay the dragon that is in the sea." (27:1)

Our word *leviathan* derives from a similar-sounding Hebrew word that means "serpent" or "dragon," and arose from an earlier root meaning "to turn" or "to twist." Apparently the name *Leviathan* shares a linguistic ancestor with *Lothan,* a seven-headed monster described by texts from the ancient coastal kingdom of Ugarit in western Syria. This monster met a fate similar to Leviathan's, but at the hands of the god Baal.

After the word *leviathan* entered English via translations of the Bible, this word's meaning expanded over time to denote any huge marine animal, such as the whale. It also acquired the even more abstract sense of "something similarly immense."

LIMACINE

To describe anyone or anything as "sluglike" or "resembling or pertaining to snails," the word you want is *limacine*. (As in "When are you going to put aside your limacine ways and start giving me a little help around here?") It's from *limax,* the Latin word for slug or snail, and can be pronounced in a variety of ways, perhaps the easiest of which rhymes with "lima bean."

Limacine apparently stems from a prehistoric root meaning

"slimy," as do the words *slime* and *slick*. The Latin word *limax* also gave us the mathematician's term *limaçon* ("LIM-uh-sun"), which describes a kind of curve that somewhat resembles a snail. It was so named by seventeenth-century mathematician Blaise Pascal, who appropriated the French word *limaçon,* which originally meant "snail shell" or "spiral staircase." See COCHLEA.

LIONEL See LEO.

LOBSTER

There's an oversize insect skittering about inside the word *lobster*. It seems the ancient Romans applied the name *locusta* to both the insect we call a *locust* as well as the crustacean we call a *lobster*—a sea creature that does look a little like an oversize version of the insect, especially if you've been away at sea for too long. Speakers of Old English apparently adopted their own insect-inspired version of this name—*loppestre*—a word possibly influenced by the Old English word *loppe,* meaning "spider," and applied it to this spidery ocean dweller.

Many animal names illustrate this linguistic tendency to describe the new and unfamiliar by comparing it to something known. The stocky, burrowing mammal called an *aardvark,* for example, has a name that describes it quite literally. *Aardvark* comes from Dutch words that literally mean "earth-pig." The *aard-* in aardvark is an etymological relative of the English word *earth,* and the *vark,* the word for pig, is a descendant of Latin *porcus,* and relative of such English words as *pork* and *porcine.* The same piggy root gave us *porpoise*—literally "pig-fish"—the linguistic offspring of the Latin words *porcus* and *piscis* (fish), which is a relative of the astrological sign *Pisces*. See PISCINE. The same idea inspired the German word for porpoise, which is *Meer-schwein*—literally "ocean-swine."

Another example: *hyena*. The ancient Greeks called this dog-like animal a *hyaina*, a name that in turn derives from the Greek word *hys*, meaning "swine"—apparently because the hyena's distinctively bristly mane resembles the coarse hair on the back of a hog. (For another "piggy back" word, see PORCELAIN.)

LOUSY

There's an infestation of lice in the word *lousy*, which originally meant literally "infested with lice." But because the state of being *pediculous* (or "lice-infested," from the Latin *pediculus*, meaning "louse") is decidedly unpleasant, the word *lousy* soon became a synonym for "vile," "crummy," or otherwise "inferior" or "unpleasant." See GRUBBY.

The "swarming" nature of lice infestation has inspired a common slang use of this word as well. Since at least the 1800s, speakers of American English sometimes have used the word *lousy* as an adjective describing something in abundance, as in "That trophy wife is always just *lousy* with diamonds, even at the swimming pool."

The Greek word for louse, *phteir,* produced the medical term for "an infestation of crab lice," *phthiriasis,* pronounced "thih-RYE-uh-sis." (From the sixteenth century right though the end of the nineteenth, phthiriasis was popularly called the *lousy disease* or the *lousy evil*.)

And if you want to describe someone as "louse eating," you would call him or her *phthirophagous,* pronounced "thye-RAH-fugg-us," and sometimes spelled *phtheirophagous*. You don't hear this word that often in our own culture, of course, but it did appear in an 1899 issue of the *British Medical Journal,* which included the intriguing observation, "Lice caused little inconvenience and afforded employment to the phteirophagous natives." See **NITPICK**. And for another animal word that involves eating strange things, see **PICA**.

LOWELL

The name *Lowell* means "wolf cub." It derives from Old French *louvel,* a diminutive of *lou,* which goes all the way back to the Latin word for wolf, *lupus.* See **LUPINE**.

LUPINE

Etymologically speaking, the *lupine* blossom gets a bad rap. This flower, which thrives in poor soil, gets its name from the Latin word *lupus,* or "wolf," because of the erroneous belief that it "wolfs" nutrients out of the earth. In reality, however, the opposite is true: Lupine is a nitrogen-fixing plant, which means that it actually increases soil fertility by converting nitrogen into a form that other plants can use.

The word *lupine* is also an adjective that describes someone who is "ruthessly predatory" or otherwise "wolflike." The Latin wolf-word *lupus* prowls around in several other languages as well, including Spanish, where a wolf is a *lobo,* and the name *López* belongs to the same linguistic family. It also produced the French word for "wolf," *loup,* which is part of the picturesque French idiom for "being torn between holding on and letting go": *tener le loup par les oreilles*—literally, "to hold the wolf by the ears."

Latin *lupus* was also borrowed whole into English as the name for a disease that attacks the skin with particularly wolflike voraciousness. As a late-sixteenth-century medical text put it, "Lupus is a malignant vlcer quickly consuming the neather parts; and it it very hungry like vnto a woolfe." See LYCANTHROPE.

LUPUS See LUPINE.

LYCANTHROPE

The Greek words for "wolf," *lukos,* and "human being," *anthropos,* lie inside the term *lycanthropy,* usually defined as a form of insanity characterized by beastly behavior which is marked by a changed voice, acts, and appetites both depraved and voracious. A *lycanthrope,* or a person afflicted with lycanthropy, suffers from the delusional belief that he or she is a wolf or other wild animal.

The word *lycanthrope* is also a synonym for werewolf, or a spirit that has assumed the earthly form of a bloodthirsty wolf. See LYCOPODIUM.

LYCOPODIUM

The name of the moss called *lycopodium* is a Latinized form of the Greek words *lukos,* "wolf," and *podion,* "little foot," an allusion to the fact that the roots of this moss look remarkably like a wolf's paw.

The spores of *lycopodium* form a fine yellow powder that makes a dramatic flash when tossed into a flame. This substance, also known as *vegetable brimstone* or *witches' meal,* was long used in theatrical productions to create stage lightning. It's also been used as an ingredient in fireworks. Because this powder is also water repellent, *lycopodium* also has been put to use as a coating for pills and surgical gloves. See LYCANTHROPE.

LYTTA See ALYSSUM.

M

MAH JONGG

This game, which is rather like rummy but is played with tiles rather than cards, originated in China where it remains wildly popular. It features 144 small engraved tiles marked with several categories, such as "flowers" and "winds." According to some authorities the name *mah jongg* comes from a dialectal version of a Chinese word for sparrow, *máquè,* a bird depicted on one of the tiles.

MARSHAL

Originally, the term *marshal* applied specifically to someone who worked in stables, looking after horses and making sure they were properly shod. Speakers of Middle English adapted this horsey word from its Old French counterpart, *mareschal,* a word with roots in a Germanic compound meaning "horse-servant." (In fact, the *mar-* or "horse," of *marshal* is etymologically related to *mare,* the modern English word for a female horse.)

Over time, the title of *marshal* acquired additional status, eventually denoting a "high official of the royal court in charge of the cavalry." Later its meaning extended further still to a variety of specific military and law-enforcement positions. Thus the development of the word *marshal* roughly parallels that of another word that originated in the idea of a horse-helper—*constable*.

In addition, its meaning of "military officer" also led to the verb *to marshal,* which originally meant "to direct troops" and now more generally means "to arrange, direct, and organize" any number of people or things. See CONSTABLE.

MAVERICK

Samuel A. Maverick was a nineteenth-century lawyer who moved from New England to Texas and went into politics. He became the mayor of San Antonio and a member of the state legislature. After accepting a herd of cattle in payment for a debt, Maverick also became a rancher on a 385,000-acre spread. Because cattle often roamed free in those days, ranchers branded them to avoid theft and ownership disputes. Maverick, however, chose not to brand his own livestock, and earned a measure of notoriety for doing so. Soon ranchers were calling any unbranded animal a *maverick,* and the meaning of this word eventually came to extend to any type of strong-willed nonconformist, and particularly to a politician not "branded" by special interests. See GOBBLEDYGOOK.

MAWKISH

The word *mawkish* usually describes anything excessively sweet, as in "Unfortunately, the last thing Agatha needed at that moment was a mawkish greeting card—particularly one signed with a smiley face." In its earliest sense, however, the word *mawk-*

ish described someone who was "squeamish" or "inclined to sickness," or something that had a "nauseating or faintly sick taste." The early sense of ickiness in the word derives from the obsolete English word *mawk,* which means "maggot." Over time, mawkish lost its grubby grossness, but kept its nauseating connotations, and now simply means "feebly sentimental" or "faintly icky-tasting." See GRUBBY.

MELDROP

From the "Isn't It Nice to Know There's a Word For It?" Department: The word *meldrop* means "a drop of mucus at the end of the nose." This handy word derives from Old Norse *méldropi,* which means "a drop or foam from a horse's mouth."

MELISSA

The inspiration for this popular name is the Greek word *melissa,* which literally means "honeybee." There is some evidence that the Greek word *melissa* is itself a combination of words that mean "honey-licker." If so, that would make the *mel-* in *melissa* an etymological relative of such honeyed words as *marmalade* and *mellifluous.* Another feminine name with a buzz is *Deborah,* from the Hebrew word for "bee." See DESERET.

MERLOT

Peer into a glass of this dark red wine, and you just might be able to make out the shape of a bird. The word *merlot* is French for young blackbird. The wine is supposedly so named because of the dark color of the grapes used to make it. The word *merlot* is also a relative of the word *merle,* which in both English and French, means "blackbird." See **KOSOVO.**

MEWS

The horses and carriages belonging to the British royal family are kept in London at a set of stables called the *Royal Mews.* The name *mews* alludes to an animal—although not to horses (or to the sound made by kittens). Originally, a mew was a cage for keeping hawks, especially when the birds were molting, or *mewing.* The Royal Mews is so named because these stables are built on the site where the royal family's hawks once were housed.

The falconry term to *mew,* in "to molt or shed feathers," derives from the Latin word *mutare,* which means "to change." Thus these words are relatives of such terms as *mutate* and *commute,* both of which also involve the idea of "change." Similarly, the expression *in mew* or *in the mew* means literally "in the process of molting," or in a figurative sense "to be in a process of transformation." Thomas Jefferson used the latter sense when he was writing about the fledgling United States of America, and recalled that "Our present government was *in the mew,* passing from Confederation to Union." See **FLEDGLING.**

As a verb, *mew* or *mew up* came to mean to "shut away" or "confine." One of the earliest (and most chilling) recorded examples of this comes from a fifteenth-century Frenchman's book written to instruct his daughters on proper courtly behavior: "Euery woman that disobeyed . . . her husbonde . . . shulde be mued alle a year [Every woman that disobeyed her husband should be mewed all a year]." As a noun, *mew* also came to denote "a pen for fattening poultry," and more generally, a place of confinement or concealment for anyone, voluntary or otherwise.

In addition, the word *mews,* usually singular despite the final *s,* came to apply not just to "molting places for hawks," but to "stables for horses as well as carriages." In London, these stables were usually grouped around a yard, alley, or other open spaces throughout the city. As the use of horses as a mode of transportation began to go the way of the buggy whip, these structures were converted to residential apartments. But the name stuck.

MIDGET

A *midge* is a tiny gnatlike fly. The name of this insect comes from the Old English word for it, *mycg.* (Thus the midge's name is a distant relative of the Latin word for fly, *musca,* as well as its Spanish descendant, *mosca,* and its diminutive, *mosquito.* The Latin word *musca* is also part of the ophthalmologist's term *musca volitans.* This term, which literally means "a fly flying about," is the medical name for "floaters," those little bits of cells that sometime appear to be drifting around in one's field of vision, a little like silent microscopic flies.)

The diminutive of the English word *midge* is the term *midget,* first recorded in the mid-nineteenth century. According to *American Heritage Dictionary,* the word *midget* is considered offensive when applied to a person who is abnormally small in size. This insect-inspired word is properly used in other contexts however, such as *midget golf,* a synonym for *miniature golf.*

MOSQUITO. See MIDGE.

MOUTON ENRAGÉ

This French phrase was adopted into English for the best of reasons—simply because we couldn't have said it better ourselves. A *mouton enragé*, according to the *Oxford English Dictionary*, is "a normally calm person who has become suddenly enraged or violent." As in "No one in the office ever dreamed that an innocent little comment about Wally's favorite snow dome would turn the guy into such a mouton enragé." Literally meaning an "angry sheep," this term is an etymological relative of the word *mutton*. See MOUTONÉE.

MOUTONNÉE

Sometimes written without the accent mark, the word *moutonnée* is a geological term that means "rounded like a sheep's back." It's used to describe rocks that have been shaped by glacial action, and derives from the French expression *roche moutonnée*, which literally means "a rock made fleecy." See MUTT.

MUNDUNGUS

The word *mundungus* means "stinky tobacco," but its origin is even more odoriferous. The word is a joking adaptation of the Spanish word *mondongo*, which means "tripe"—or, in other words, the stomach lining of various animals sometimes cooked and served as food.

Mundungus made its first appearance in English in the seventeenth century. Sir Walter Scott used this redolent term in 1824, describing someone's "jet black cutty pipe, from which she soon sent . . . clouds of vile mundungus vapour." Fifteen years later, another writer shuddered at the memory of someone who was, in his words, "offending the nostrils of all misocapnists with the fumes of his mundungus." (*Misocapnist?* This handy English term derives from Greek words that literally mean "someone who hates smoke.")

MURINE

Murine may be the name of a brand of eye drops, but the non-trademarked English word *murine,* with an accent on the first syllable, means "of or resembling mice." Murine can also refer to something caused by mice, such as *a murine plague.* A derivative of the Latin term *murinus,* meaning "of mice," the word is in fact an etymological relative of the English word *mouse.*

MUSCLE

Clench your fist to make your biceps pop up, and you'll see why we call it a *muscle.* The ancient Romans referred to a muscle as a *musculus*—literally, a "little mouse," perhaps because of the way a twitching muscle under the skin resembles a little mouse under a blanket. Borrowing on that same idea, English speakers long ago used the word *mouse* as a synonym for muscle. Until at least the end of the nineteenth century, the English word *mouse* also denoted certain muscular cuts of meat. See MYOSOTIS.

MUSE

The verb *muse,* as in "to ponder," may allude to the distracted look of an animal sniffing the air. Some authorities suspect it's from an Old French term for snout, *muse* (a relative of our own word *muzzle*). This word gave the rise to Middle French *muser*, which means "to stare stupidly"—and, in its earliest sense, specified the way a hunting dog sniffs when unsure about a scent.

MUSTELINE

If you want to say that someone is like a weasel, call him *musteline*. Deriving from the Latin word *mustela,* meaning "weasel," musteline applies to animals in the furry family *Mustelidae,* which includes skunks, badgers, otters, minks, and martens. Besides its specific sense of "resembling a weasel," *musteline* can also mean "tawny or brown, like the coat of a weasel in summertime." See TAUPE.

MUTT

Because sheep are traditionally assumed to be stupid, the word *muttonhead* came to be applied to anyone considered similarly dull witted. In the early 1900s, speakers of English sheared off this word's final two syllables, and began using *mutt* to refer to people rather than animals. Then in 1904, the *Oxford English Dictionary* explains, a writer contemptuously applied the word *mutt* to a horse. Two years later, another used it to refer to a dog, exclaiming, "A fellow can't leave nothin' on his bed without that mutt chawin' it up!" Today this word inspired by sheep meat refers to either "a mixed-breed dog" or "a stupid person." (See MOUTONNÉE.)

MYOSOTIS

A little mouse lends its ear to the scientific name for that tiny flower also called a *forget-me-not*. The name *myosotis* derives from Greek, where *myosotis* means "mouse-ear," and refers to this flower's small, hairy, rounded leaves. In English, myosotis is sometimes called *mouse-ear* or *myosote,* as in an 1890 poem that includes the evocative line: "And laden barges float / By banks of myosote."

The *myo-,* or "mouse," in *myosotis* is a linguistic relative of such words as *mouse* and *muscle.* The *-otis,* or "ear," is from the same root that gives us the word *otitis,* or "inflammation of the ear," and *otoscope,* the name of the device used for seeing into the ear.

Incidentally, *myomancy* is the practice of "attempting to tell the future by observing the movements of mice." This was apparently a popular activity in ancient times, and may explain why Isaiah 66:17 includes the mouse in a list of abominations associated with pagan practices. See MUSCLE.

MYRMIDON

Pronounced either "MURR-muh-don" or "MURR-muh-dn," the word *myrmidon* means an "unscrupulous underling or follower who faithfully executes a superior's commands without question." As in "Congressman Whitterick got into trouble because all along, his myrmidons were afraid to point out that his self-righteous stump speech wasn't playing well with the public." (*Whitterick*? It's an old term for "weasel," possibly deriving from the words *white* and *rat.*)

Literally, however, the word *myrmidon* is crawling with ants. This term was inspired by the ancient story of the Myrmidons, a warlike tribe from ancient Thessaly. As described in *The Iliad,* these soldiers faithfully followed Achilles into battle at Troy and fought tirelessly. The name *Myrmidon* itself derives from the Greek word *myrmēx,* which means "ant." It seems that much earlier, an angry goddess had sent a series of nasty plagues to ravage the ancestral island of the Myrmidons. The island's streams turned foul, snakes overran the land, and huge numbers of people and animals perished. Now desperate, their king took the matter to Zeus, imploring him to repopulate the realm with as many men as there were ants crawling upon a tree in a nearby sacred grove. Zeus, who also happened to be the king's father, obliged with a big flash of lightning. The next day, the plagues were gone, and all the ants on that tree were transformed into fierce fighting men. To commemorate their miraculous metamorphosis, the king named his warriors *Myrmidónes,* the source of our own word *Myrmidon,* which can also be spelled with a lowercase *m.*

Today the Greek word for ant is preserved in several scientific words, including *myrmecology,* which denotes the study of ants. Similarly, the anteaters are classified in the scientific family *Myrmecophagidae,* which literally means "ant-eaters." Meanwhile, the Latin word for ant, *formica,* appears in several other creepy words. See **FORMICATION**.

N

N

The Phoenician and Semitic alphabets include a letter that goes by the name *nun,* which means "fish." The Greeks adapted it for their own letter *nû,* and eventually it found its way into the Roman alphabet as N. The root of all these letters is an Egyptian hieroglyph that consists of a wavy line, which originally meant "sea" or "fish." See Q.

NEST EGG

At least as early as the seventeenth century, it was common to leave a ceramic egg in a hen's nest, all the better to encourage her to keep laying eggs there. As a 1614 manual on animal husbandry advised, "You shall gather you Egges up once a day, and leaue in the nest but the nest-Egge, and no more."

Less than a century later, people were applying the term *nest egg* figuratively, to mean "something set out either to confuse or to attract." Later still, the expression came to mean "a reserve of extra cash set aside"—a reserve intended, like the ersatz egg, to result in the acquisition of more.

NICHE

The word *niche,* meaning "a recess in a wall," or in a figurative sense, "a place particularly suited for someone's talents or interests," derives from the Old French verb *nichier,* which means "to make a nest." *Niche* is thought to derive from the Latin word *nidus,* which means "nest" and derives from a prehistoric compound that literally meant "the place where the bird sits down," and is also the source, ultimately, of the word *nest* itself.

The word Latin *nidus* also gave us the English word *nestle,* meaning "to make a nest." The word *nidus* itself now nestles in the English language as well, where it's pronounced "NYE-duss," and serves as a zoologists' term for nest. The word *nidus* also can be used figuratively, as in a nineteenth-century travelogue that characterized the Sorbonne as having once been "the *nidus* of pedantry."

The verb *to nidify* (rhymes with "humidify") means "to build a nest" (as in "Arnold had always prided himself on being footloose and fancy-free, but ever since meeting Robin, he had been feeling the urge to nidify.") The word *nidicolous* means "living in a nest," and the adjective *nidifugous* describes birds whose offspring are so well-developed after hatching that they leave the nest shortly thereafter. Latin *nidus* is also the source of that collective noun referring to a flock of pheasants, which is properly called either a *nye* or *nide.*

The linguistic descendants hatched from the Latin word *nidus* also include what may be the most picturesque term in any language for that pesky impediment in the road, a pothole. In France, these irritating craters are named for a critter: there a pothole is called a *nid-de-poule*—a hen's nest.

NITPICK

The word *nit* means "the egg of a louse," and comes from an Old English word, *hnitu*. It's a relative of similarly nitlike words for these insect eggs in several languages: in Dutch, it's *neet*; German, *Niss*; Polish, *gnida*; Czech, *knida*; Norwegian, *gnit*; Swedish, *gnet*; Danish, *gnid*; and Icelandic, *nit*.

The word *nitpick,* then, literally means to pick off these little buggers. Fortunately, we now use the word *nitpick* primarily in a figurative sense, as in "to be excessively critical" or "to carp about trivial details." But although real live *nits* have been around forever, and our name for them goes back to at least the ninth century, the word *nitpick* is of relatively recent vintage, having first been recorded in 1951. See LOUSY.

NOM DE PLUME See PLUME.

OCARINA

This small wind instrument takes its name from a diminutive of the Italian word *oca,* or "goose." That's because the egg-shaped ocarina has a mouthpiece shaped like a goose's beak. Incidentally, the Italian word *oca,* is a descendant of the Latin word for bird, *avis,* which makes *ocarina* a relative of all those other bird words, like *aviation.* See **AUSPICES.**

OOLONG

The strong, dark tea from China and Taiwan called *oolong* has a beastly name. It derives from the Chinese term *wulong*—or literally, "black dragon."

OPHRA

The feminine name *Ophra,* and its variant, *Ofra,* derive from a Hebrew word that means "young deer." (Note that these names are apparently no relation to the similarly spelled feminine name, *Oprah.* This name's most famous owner, Oprah Winfrey, was named for Orpah, who in Hebrew scripture was the daughter-in-law of Naomi. However, due to a misspelling on her birth certificate, she ended up with the name *Oprah*.)

ORNITHOPHILIST

The word *ornithophilist* means "bird lover." The word *ornitholophilist* derives from the Greek words *ornis,* meaning "bird," and *philos,* meaning "lover." See **PHILIP**.

Similarly, flowers that entice hummingbirds to sip their nectar and spread their pollen are said to be *ornithophilous,* a word that literally means "bird-loving." The study of birds is called *ornithology,* and *ornithocopros* is a fancy name for "bird dropping," as in "Er, don't look now, but I believe that's a bit of ornithocopros on your shoulder." Then there's *ornithocoprophilous* (pronounced "OAR-ni-tho-kuh-PRAH-fill-us"), a term that describes something that is literally "bird-dung loving." Certain lichens, for example, are said to be ornithocoprophilous because they do especially well when exposed to bird droppings.

ORNITHOSCOPY See AUSPICES.

ORSON

The name *Orson* is a borrowing of the Old Norman French word for bear cub. The ursine ancestor of Orson is the Latin word *ursus,* which also means "bear." See **URSINE**.

OVINE

Usually pronounced "OH-vyne," the adjective *ovine* applies to anyone or anything with sheeplike characteristics. You might say, for example, "My, isn't her new boyfriend ovine?"—that is, if the fellow seems timid, submissive, or easily led or swayed. This useful term comes to us courtesy of the Latin word *ovis,* which means "sheep," and also gave us the word *ewe.* Incidentally, if you ever get tired of using the phrase *a flock of sheep,* you can always substitute the shorter synonym, *oviary.*

OXLIP See COWSLIP.

P

PALOMA See PALOMINO.

PALOMINO

Here's a horse that is named for a bird. We borrowed the word *palomino* from Spanish, where it means "of or resembling a dove"—a name thought to allude to the pale color of this horse's golden coat and cream-colored mane.

The Spanish *palomino*, in turn, derives from the Latin word *palumbinus*, or "resembling a dove." From the same root comes the word *palumbino*, the name of a variety of "dove gray" Italian marble.

The Spanish word for dove, *paloma*, also gave us the feminine name *Paloma*. This bird nestles inside the name of *Palomar Mountain* in California, home to a famous observatory; its name means "place frequented by doves." The Spanish word *paloma* is also a picturesque slang term for popcorn. In Mexico, these puffed kernels are sometimes called *palomitas*, or "little doves." See COLUMBINE.

PANACHE

The word *panache* means "dash," "flamboyance," or "verve," but in its earliest sense it referred to part of a bird. This word's Latin ancestor, *pinnaculum,* means "little feather or wing."

This Latin bird word found its way into French as *panache,* where it originally meant "a plume of feathers," such as those found on a helmet or a fancy headdress, and later came to mean more generally "a grand manner," "swagger," or "flair."

The French word *panache* proved so useful for expressing just this notion that the speakers of English simply adopted it whole. As in, "What the pianist lacked in talent, she tried to make up for with a sequined gown and plenty of panache." See PLUME.

PASS THE BUCK See BUCK.

PASTOR

We speak today of a *pastor* and his or her "flock," but there was a time when pastors really did spend their days looking after flocks of real live sheep. The Latin word *pastor* means "shepherd"—literally "a feeder"—and for hundreds of years, this word's English counterpart could refer to either "a herder of sheep," or the kind of "spiritual shepherd" who pastors a church.

The Latin word *pastor* derives from a much older root that means "feeder," making *pastor* a relative of such bucolic words as *pasture* ("the place where the flocks feed"), *pastoral* ("a word that describes art or literature that celebrates rural life"), and the word *repast* ("a meal," from the Latin word *repascere,* "to feed regularly").

132

PAVILION

Here's a word with a butterfly inside: The word *pavilion* comes from the Latin word *papilio,* which the Romans originally used to mean "butterfly" or "moth." Later they applied this name to a type of tent with flaps that resembled a butterfly's outstretched wings. The Latin word *papilio* eventually produced our own word *pavilion,* a term that first denoted "a tent," then "a temporary shelter," and eventually extended to more permanent ones— specifically, "a light, usually open structure, often found at parks or fairs." As in "What do you say we waltz on over to the edge of the pavilion and then take our own tour of the premises?" (And yes, our word *pavilion* is an etymological relative of the French name for the same insect, *papillon.*)

PAVONINE

To describe someone who acts like a peacock, or to describe something iridescent like a peacock's coloration, the word you want is *pavonine* (PAV-oh-nyne or PAV-oh-nin). It's from the Latin name for this showy bird, *pavo.*

PECULATE See PECULIAR.

PECULIAR

There's a herd in this word; its Latin root, *pecu,* means "a herd of cattle." It used to be that a common measure of wealth was how many cattle one owned. Later, the Romans' word for cattle, *pecu,* naturally inspired their word for money, *pecunia.*

(You can still hear this Latin word for money jingling inside several English words, including the terms *pecuniary,* or "having to do with money," and *impecunious,* or "lacking money.") From this same word herd comes the English term *peculate,* which means "to embezzle" (from the Latin *peculari,* literally, "to make public property private"), and *peculator,* "embezzler." Then there's *pecudiculture,* which, as you might guess, is a fancy term for "the raising of cattle."

Similarly, the Latin word *peculiaris* meant "of private property." In a more abstract sense, the word *peculiaris* came to mean "of one's own." This idea that led to the modern English word *peculiar,* which means "belonging uniquely or primarily to one person or group."

Incidentally, the same prehistoric root that produced these bovine words also sired several Germanic ones, including the English word *fee,* which once meant either "cattle" or "possessions," and eventually acquired its cattle-less modern sense of "money received or paid."

PECUNIARY See PECULIAR.

PEDIGREE

The word *pedigree* has a fascinating pedigree, one that involves the name of a tall leggy bird. While we call this bird a *crane,* the French call it a *grue.* A few hundred years ago, the Old French term for the "foot of a crane" was *pie de grue.*

Now, picture a genealogical chart with its three-line diagrams indicating who plus who begat whom. Speakers of Old French started calling this /|\-shaped figure a *pie de grue*—the linguistic ancestor of our own *pedigree*. Incidentally, another bird's foot is fossilized in a German term for quotation marks—*Gansefüsschen,* or literally, "little geese's feet." See GERANIUM.

PELARGONIUM

By the sixteenth century, English speakers were using the word *geranium,* a name that refers to the resemblance between a flower's pointed seed pod and the shape of a crane's bill. See GERANIUM. In the nineteenth century, scientists applied another bird word to a different flower with a similar-looking seed pod. They called this flower a *pelargonium,* a name adapted from the Greek word for "stork," *pelargos.* See ANTIPELARGY.

PEN

Here's another bird word: Just as the quill pen preceded modern ballpoints and felt tips, the Latin word *penna,* or "feather," is the linguistic forerunner of our word *pen.* Thus the word *pen* is an etymological relative of such words as *penne,* the name of the quill-shaped Italian pasta. See PANACHE and PLUME.

PENCIL

Among the many names the ancient Romans bestowed upon male genitalia was the Latin term *penis,* a word that, strangely enough, means "tail." However odd that may seem, we borrowed the word *penis* into English anyway. (A similar notion is apparently at work in the dual meaning of a modern German word for tail, *Schwanz,* which is also slang for penis.)

There's also a little Latin *penis,* or tail, embedded in our word *pencil.* Our word for this writing instrument derives from the Latin word *penicillus,* which literally means "little tail," but was also used to mean "paintbrush," because of their similarity in appearance. In 1591, for example, a writer made this observation about writing methods used in the Far East: "All the Chineans, Iaponians, and Cauchin Chineans do write right downwards, and they do write with a fine pensill made of dogs or cats haire." (Again, a similar idea is preserved in German, where the related word *Pinsel* means "paintbrush," and the graphite writing instrument with an eraser at the end is instead called a *Bleistift.*)

Similarly, the antibiotic *penicillin* is so called because it comes from the mold that goes by the scientific name *pencillium* because of the brushlike filaments that support its tiny spores. (For more tales about tails, see QUEUE.)

PENICILLIN See PENCIL.

PENIS See PENCIL.

PERISTERONIC

If you need a word that means "suggestive of pigeons" or "having to do with pigeons," there's always *peristeronic.* It comes from the Greek word for dove or pigeon, *peristera.* You might say that a person who is pigeon-toed has a *peristeronic gait,* for example, or employ this word to evocative effect as a writer did in 1931, describing a conversation that was "punctuated with polite little peristeronic sounds." See COLUMBINE.

PHILIP

The name *Philip* literally means "horse-loving," and derives from the Greek words *hippos,* for horse, and *philos,* a term for loving or friend.

The *hippos,* or "horse," inside the name *Philip* hides within a few other words as well. One of them is *hippopotamus,* which comes from Greek words that literally mean "river horse." (The *potamos,* or river, in the name of the *hippopotamus,* also resides in the word *Mesopotamia,* the "fertile crescent" that lies in the middle—or in Greek, *mesos*—of the Tigris and Euphrates rivers.) A horse also rears its head in the name of the botanical genus *Hippeastrum,* which includes the lovely flower, amaryllis. The reason: for a few days before the amaryllis bud opens, the two pointed leaves enclosing it stick up in a way that resembles a horse's ears.

The term *philippic,* however, is hardly a loving one. This word means "a bitter verbal attack" and commemorates the impassioned diatribes by the Greek orator Demosthenes against King Philip II of Macedonia.

PHTEIROPHAGOUS See LOUSY.

PICA

The magpie, a bird with a reputation for eating just about anything, inspired this term for "an abnormal craving for non-food substances," such as clay, dirt, chalk, and even laundry starch or burnt matches." In fact, we borrowed the Latin name for this bird, *pica,* directly into English.

This craving sometimes occurs in people suffering from malnutrition, and occasionally in pregnant women. In parts of Africa, pregnant women are known to nibble from mineral-rich termite mounds, and in eastern Guatemala, the faithful purchase and consume holy clay tablets, which are said to possess powers to induce or nurture pregnancy.

Another word for *pica* is *geophagy,* which comes from Greek words that literally mean "earth-eating." See PIEBALD.

PICINE

Need a word for "woodpecker-like"? Look no further than *picine* (rhymes with "my sign"). It's also the Latin word for woodpecker, and will do quite nicely if you ever need to say something like "When he opened the envelope and pulled out yet another rejection slip, Jason turned to the wall and engaged in picine behavior, which seemed to relieve his frustration, but left a bruise on his forehead."

PIEBALD

The black-and-white patches on a magpie inspired this term for similar markings on other animals, such as horses. The word *piebald* is a combination of this bird's nickname, *pie,* and *bald,* a word that sometimes denotes white coloration on an animal, as in the term *bald eagle*.

PINION

To pinion someone means "to bind his arms or hands," or otherwise restrain him. In its earliest sense, though, the word *pinion* was a noun that meant "all or part of of a bird's wing," and *to pinion* meant "to clip or bind the feathers of a bird's wing to prevent it from flying." Pinion derives from the Latin word *pinna,* which means "feather" or "wing." The Latin word *pinna* also survives intact in English as an anatomical term for the outer ear—literally, the "wing" on either side of one's head. See **PANACHE**.

Incidentally, these winged words are etymologically unrelated to the *pinion* in a car—in other words, a "small cogwheel that engages with a larger one or with a rack" (as in *rack-and-pinion steering*). This type of *pinion* has a name deriving from an Old French word *peigne,* which denotes a similarly "toothed" object, a "comb."

PINNA See PINION.

PISCINE

Pronounce it "PYE-seen" or "PISS-yne" (or in Britain, "PISS-in" or "piss-SEEN")—any way you say it, *piscine* means "pertaining to or resembling fish." It derives from the Latin word *piscis,* meaning "fish," and is not to be confused with the differently pronounced *picine,* which has to do with woodpeckers. See PICINE.

From the Latin word for fish comes the name for the astrological sign *Pisces,* as well as the English word *piscina,* an ecclesiastical term for a basin with a drain used to carry away water used in ceremonial practices. (In Spanish, Italian, and Portuguese, a *piscina* is a "swimming pool.") Something that's "fish-shaped" is *pisciform* ("PYE-sih-form" or "PISS-ih-form"), and if you eat fish, you're piscivorous ("pye-SIHV-urr-us" or "pih-SIHV-urr-us"). Something abounding in fish is said to be *pisculent,* as in "My, what a pisculent pond you have there!" If something is "fishy," you can describe it with the rare and obsolete adjective *piscose.* See ICHTHYIC.

PLUME

The offspring of the Latin word *pluma,* or "soft feather," the English word *plume* has several meanings. We use it literally in the expression *peacock's plume* and metaphorically when we speak of a *plume of smoke.* The Latin word *pluma* also produced the Spanish word *pluma,* which literally means "feather," but also "inkpen," the connection being the early use of quills as writing instruments. The same occurs in French, where *plume* can mean either "pen" or "feather," and a *nom de plume* is a "pseudonym"— or in its most literal sense, a "pen name." See PANACHE.

And in case you ever need a rhyme for *unicorn,* there's always *plumicorn,* an ornithological term from the Latin *pluma* that means "one of the pair of hornlike feathers that makes an owl appear to have horns or ears." See CORNUCOPIA.

PLUMICORN See PLUME.

POPINJAY

Originally meaning "parrot," the word *popinjay* is now a handy term for "a pretentious blabbermouth" or "vain person given to empty prattle." The word is an adaptation of an Old French word for parrot, *papegai,* which derives from the Spanish *papagayo* and ultimately goes back to an Arabic word, *babaghā,* which is probably an onomatopoetic term evoking the cry of a chattering bird.

(For another word that calls to mind a prattling parrot, see PSITTACINE.)

PORCINE See PORCELAIN.

PORCELAIN

There's a "porker" in *porcelain,* the name of a smooth white ceramic used for making fine dinnerware—although it takes a little digging to find it. The story goes like this: When the thirteenth-century Venetian explorer Marco Polo brought examples of it back from the Far East, his countrymen were struck by the way this shiny, translucent material resembled the glossy surface of a cowrie shell, or in Italian, a *porcellana.* So they applied the name of the shell to this unfamiliar substance, a name that eventually found its way into French as *porcelaine* and later into English as *porcelain.*

Now, here's where it gets a little zoologically complicated. The Italian name for the cowrie shell comes from the word *porcella,* which means "a little female pig." The word *porcella* derives from the Latin word *porcus,* which gives us such piggy words as *pork, porcine* ("piglike"), and *porpoise* (literally, "pig-fish"). Although etymologists are sure of this much, the question remains: What's the connection between a female pig and a cowrie shell? Here the word historians differ. Some speculate that Italians named the cowrie shell *porcellana* because its rounded outer surface resembles the back of a little pig. This explanation, as Craig M. Carver notes in his excellent volume, *A History of English in Its Own Words,* is bolstered by the fact that people have long made toy pigs out of cowrie shells, using the shell for the body and adding putty appendages.

The other explanation, however, is a bit racier. This one holds that the connection between sows and cowrie shells is the fact that the opening of a cowrie shell resembles a sow's vulva. This explanation is certainly plausible as well, and perhaps it is bolstered by the fact that, in English, the cowrie shell also goes by the erotically charged name *Venus shell,* presumably because of a similar resemblance.

PORPOISE See PISCINE.

PSITTACINE

Pronounced (SITT-uh-syn), this word describes anything "resembling, characteristic of, or pertaining to parrots." It's from the Latin word *psittacus,* which means "parrot," and can refer literally to a parrot, or describe parrotlike behavior. As in "To run for office these days requires a psittacine willingness to repeat the same old phrases, again and again and again and again."

The *Oxford English Dictionary* cites one writer who in 1938 used the handy related word *psittacism* when wryly observing that "Speaking without knowing is called *psittacism,* but it is a practice not confined to parrots." *Psittacosis* is an infectious disease of parrots and similar birds that can be transmitted to humans. Also called *parrot fever,* it causes high fever, a nasty headache, and symptoms similar to pneumonia. See **POPINJAY**.

PSITTACISM, PSITTACOSIS See PSITTACINE.

PSYLLIUM

The packaging on high-fiber breakfast cereals often boasts that these products contain the ingredient *psyllium*, a name that sounds wonderfully salubrious. Linguistically speaking, however, these cereals have "fleas." The tiny seeds called *psyllium*, which function as a natural laxative, take their name from the Greek word *psulla*, or "flea," because of their shape. Presumably cereal makers decided to go with the scientific name of this high-fiber grain rather than its more common one—*fleawort*. See PUCE.

PUCE

The source of this color name is the French word *puce*, which means "flea." The French expression *couleur puce*, or "flea color" is a reference to the color of these blood-sucking pests, perhaps to their purplish color after they have been squished. (John Donne's strange poem "The Flea" mentions someone "purpling" her nail by smashing a flea.)

For a time, *puce* was an extremely fashionable color among the members of the French court. The *Oxford English Dictionary* cites a 1776 publication in which a writer mentions a "new-fashioned flea-colored coat" and a 1794 work that refers to "a brilliant flea-brown color." *Puce* derives from the Latin for "flea," *pulex*, which also gave us the Spanish for flea, *pulga*, and the English term for flea-killer, *pulicide*. See UKULELE.

PULICIDE See PUCE.

PURPLE

In antiquity, the Phoenicians in the Mediterranean port city of Tyre were famous for producing a brilliant purple dye, one so highly prized that it was used to dye robes of royalty. The story of this dye's discovery goes back to a mythical tale about Hercules and his faithful sheepdog.

Legend had it that the two were out for a walk one day on the beach near Tyre when the dog picked up a mollusk in his teeth and bit it. When the dog's mouth turned the color of coagulated blood, Hercules realized he had found the source of a potentially lucrative product.

At any rate, the Greek name for the shellfish that yielded this dye was *porphýra*, a word that came to be applied to both the dye and the cloth it tinted. In Latin, this multipurpose word became *purpura*, which led to the Old English word *purpure*, which denoted similarly colored cloth, and in turn produced our own word for the color *purple*. (For other words that allude to a coloring made from crushed creatures, see CRIMSON, INGRAINED, PUCE, and VERMILLION.)

Q

The Roman letter Q is thought to have evolved from the Phoenician letter *qoph,* which has a name that translates as *monkey.* See X.

QUARRY

Today we often use *quarry* to mean "the object of a pursuit," as in "Law enforcement agents are now closing in on their *quarry.*" Originally, however, quarry meant something more specific and grisly—namely, the entrails of a deer given to hunting dogs as a reward for helping to track it down. Traditionally, hunters would spread out the deer's hide and then place its innards on top for the hounds to devour. This dog-pleasing pile of guts and organs was called the *quarry.*

Some etymologists suspect that the word *quarry* arose from the Latin word *cor,* meaning "heart" (a relative of the English words *courage,* as well as *cordial,* which literally means "of the heart") and was influenced by the French *cuir,* meaning "skin" or "hide." Others suspect that quarry derives more directly, via the French *cuir,* from the Latin word for skin or hide, *corium.* If the latter is true, this would make quarry a linguistic relative of *excoriate*, yet another word that originally meant something quite grisly. Although today we most often use excoriate when we speak of giving someone a verbal tongue-lashing, in its earliest sense excoriate was associated with another bloody practice; literally it meant to "pull off the hide of a beast or the skin from a person"— to "flay," in other words. (For another common expression involving deer innards, see HUMBLE PIE.)

This type of quarry, by the way, is unrelated to the kind used for excavating stone. The word *quarry* in that sense derives from a Latin root that means "a place where stone is squared," and derives from the word *quadrum*. Thus this type of quarry shares an etymological ancestor with such words as *quart* (four of which make a gallon) and *quarter* (four of which make a whole).

QUEUE

Primarily heard in Britain, the word *queue,* as in "a long line of people," stands at the end of an etymological queue stretching from the Latin word *cauda,* or "tail." We borrowed the word *queue* from French, where it also means "tail." A variation on this word is our name for the long, tapering stick used in pool or billiards, *cue.* See CODA.

R

RACHEL

The name *Rachel* comes from a Hebrew word meaning "ewe." In Hebrew scripture, Rachel was the younger, prettier sister of Leah.

Incidentally, several etymologies have been offered for the older sister's name, most often the one that says the name *Leah* comes from Hebrew for weary or weary-eyed (an allusion to the idea that she was often sorrowful, especially since her younger sister was considered far more desirable.) However, at least one source suggests that the name *Leah* derives from the Hebrew *Lē'â,* or wild ox.

RAFE See RALPH.

RALPH

The name *Ralph* is one of several masculine names in English that have a wolf prowling around inside of them. *Ralph,* along with its variants *Rafe, Raoul,* and *Raul,* arose from the Germanic name *Radulf*—a combination of *rad,* meaning "counsel," and *wulf,* the name for the lupine animal.

Similarly, the name *Randolph* is a combination of the Germanic element *rand,* or "shield-rim," and the word *wulf.* Yet another wolfish name is *Rolf,* which comes from the Germanic name *Hrodwulf,* a combination of the word *wulf* and *hrod,* which means "fame." See LUPE.

RANDOLPH See RALPH.

RAOUL, RAUL See RALPH.

RANKLE

There's a little snake coiled inside the word *rankle,* which means "to cause keen irritation or bitter resentment." This verb goes back to the Latin word *dracunculus,* the diminutive of *draco,* which means "serpent," and is the source of our term for a monster that's partly serpentine, *dragon.* Etymologists believe that the Latin word *dracunculus* developed the additional sense of "a festering sore" or "cancerous tumor," most likely because some of these sores resembled a coiled snake in appearance—and perhaps also because of their painful "bite."

In any case, the Latin word *dracunculus* gave rise to the Old French verb, *draoncler* and its variant *raoncler,* both of which mean "to fester," and passed into Middle English as the verb *ranclen.* Initially, speakers of English used this verb specifically in relation to festering sores. (In 1523, a writer observed, "His soores rankled and . . . within a shorte space after he dyed." A century later another noted, "A Leaper shut vp in a Pesthouse, ranckleth to himself, infects not others.")

As happens with many English words, however, the original, grisly sense of *rankle* drained away, leaving us mercifully with a more abstract term for describing the act of causing extreme irritation.

Incidentally, the word *dracunculus,* or "little dragon," also appears in the name of *Artemisia dracunculus,* a plant whose aromatic leaves are used to make the spice *tarragon.* Actually, it appears that the Greek word for dragon, *drakōn,* is the source of this spice's name. In ancient Greek, *drakōn* was used to denote both the serpent and the spice. No one's sure why, although several explanations have been suggested. It may be because this plant was thought to be useful in curing the venomous bites of snakes, or that the plant itself has a spicy "bite" to it. Or it may be that this plant's name alludes to the serpentine curl of its roots.

The ancient Greek plant name *drakōn* followed a rather serpentine etymological path, morphing along the way, traveling from ancient Greek into Arabic, then Medieval Greek, then Medieval Latin, and on into Middle French and finally into English, where it ended up as *tarragon.*

RARA AVIS

We adopted this expression meaning "a rare person or thing" directly from Latin, where *rara avis* literally means "rare bird." The ancient Roman poet Juvenal used this term in his famous line: *"Rara avis in terris nigroque simillima cycno,"* which means, "A rare bird on the earth, and very much like a black swan."

This image of a bird that stands out from the rest of the flock has proved compelling in other languages as well. When Russians want to say that someone is a "rare bird," for example, they use the expression *belaya vorona,* a term that literally means "a white crow." See EGREGIOUS.

REHEARSE See HEARSE.

RELAY

When the term *relay* first appeared in English in the late thirteenth century, the *Oxford English Dictionary* tells us, this word specifically referred to "a set of fresh hounds (and horses) posted to take up the chase of a deer in place of those already tired out." The word *relay* comes from the Old French term *relaier,* which means to "leave behind." It's a relative of the English word *release.*

The meaning of relay gradually extended from "a fresh team of dogs for a hunt" to "a fresh team of horses stationed at various points along a route for travellers." (For another term involving rested and ready horses, see HOBSON'S CHOICE.)

Over time the English word *relay* lost its sense of passing along a task from one set of animals to another. Today we use it primarily in the sense of passing something from one person to another, as in "How many times do I have to ask you not to relay those stupid e-mail jokes to my mailbox?"

ROAD

There's a long and winding history behind the word *road.* As early as A.D. 900, speakers of Old English used this word's ancestor, *rād,* to mean "a riding"—that is, literally, "a journey on horseback." In the sixteenth and early seventeenth centuries, later forms of the Old English word *rād* commonly meant "a hostile incursion by riders on horseback." As one writer noted in 1665, "The English . . . assailed and made incursions and Rodes upon all Spanish ships, and other places." By Shakespeare's time, the word *road* had also come to mean "the path by which people made journeys, whether hostile or not, on horseback or otherwise."

Actually, the early sense of road as "a raid on horseback" survives in the modern use of the word *inroad*; this term first referred specifically to "a hostile incursion," but is now also used in a more general sense to mean "an advance or encroachment, usually at another's expense." The "riding" word *rād* also led to the Middle English *rade,* which the Scots adapted as *raide,* meaning "a hostile incursion"—which eventually led to our own word *raid.*

ROLF See RALPH.

ROLLMOPS

The spicy, marinated fillets of herring wrapped around an onion or gherkin known as *rollmops* take their name from the German word *Mops,* which means "pug dog," and *rollen,* "to roll."

Speaking of rollmops, although the Czech word *zavinac* originally meant "rollmop," it now doubles as a synonym for the @ sign. (For the clever names for this symbol in many languages, see COCHLEA.)

ROSTRUM

Step up on a *rostrum* to make a speech and linguistically speaking you're standing on a bird's beak. (We borrowed *rostrum,* meaning "beak," directly from the Latin.) The Romans later applied this word to the curved prow of ancient ships as well, because of their beaklike shape. So what's the link between the beak and the platform?

The story goes back to 338 B.C., when a Roman consul successfully put down a rebellion by the city of Antium (now the Italian city of Anzio). Like any returning victor, the consul brought back trophies—in this case the bronze "beaks" from six of the captured enemy ships. The Romans, in turn, decided to display these *rostra* prominently, using them to decorate a platform in the Forum, where orators regularly held forth. Eventually the name of the decorations also came to apply to the place they adorned; Romans began calling that platform the *rostra*.

Speakers of English later borrowed the term *rostra* to denote any raised platform for a speaker. By the eighteenth century, however—perhaps because the Latin plural was too confusing—they switched back to the singular, *rostrum*.

ROUSE

The verb *to rouse* comes to us from the language of falconry. In the late fifteenth century, the word *rouse* alluded to the action of a hawk shaking its feathers. As a fifteenth-century writer observed, "She Rousith when she shakith all hir federis. [She rouseth when she shaketh all her feathers.]" Explained another in 1678, "*Rowze*, in Falcounry is when a Hawk lifteth up, and shaketh her self."

This sense of rising and ruffling one's feathers gradually expanded to the use of *rouse* as a hunting term meaning "to flush out game from a lair or hiding place," as well as its more metaphorical sense today of "to awaken," "startle," or "provoking."

With the addition of the intensifying prefix *a-*, the word *rouse* also formed *arouse*. The reason for such a progression from *rouse* to *arouse* is unclear, although this formation follows a pattern that has occurred with several other verbs, such as from *rise* to *arise*, as well as *wake* to *awake*, and *bide* to *abide*. See **BAT ONE'S EYES**.

RUNNER-UP

Although we usually hear the term *runner-up* in reference to beauty contests and political elections, this expression originally referred to competitions among dogs. First recorded in the early nineteenth century, this term for "a competitor who finishes second to the winner," is from the world of dog racing, where a *runner-up* originally was "a hound that comes in second in the final heat." As a text from 1890 explains, "The dog last running with the winner is called the *runner up*, because he ran through the races up to the last race without being defeated once."

SACCADE

If you've ever watched the eyes of someone reading or looking around a room, then you've seen a *saccade*. Ophthalmologists use the term for "the series of jerky little movements of the eyes when reading or changing focus from one point to another." Thomas Pynchon used this word to sensuous effect in *Gravity's Rainbow*, when describing someone who "could feel in his skin each saccade of her olive, her amber, her coffee-colored eyes."

In its earliest use, however, the word *saccade* was an equestrian term. An early eighteenth-century dictionary defined *saccade* as "a jerk or violent check which the rider gives his horse, by drawing both the reins very suddenly." This word apparently derives from an Old North French term, *saquier,* meaning "to pull or jerk violently."

SAWBUCK

A sawhorse is that familiar frame used to supports pieces of wood while sawing, its name alluding to the way its four legs make it look like a horse, albeit one that's extremely underfed. See **EASEL**. The word *sawbuck* denotes a kind of sawhorse, especially one having crossed legs. The *buck* in this case derives from the Dutch word *bok,* meaning "goat," and alludes to the way a sawbuck's legs resemble the spindly legs of a goat.

At least as early as the nineteenth century, the word *sawbuck* also has meant "a ten-dollar bill." The reason is the resemblance between a sawbuck's crossed legs and the *X* that is the Roman numeral "ten." By extension, *sawbuck* has also come to be a slang term for "a ten-year prison sentence." See BUCK.

SCAPEGOAT

Today we tend to think of a *scapegoat* as a stand-in—someone who bears blame or suffers punishment in place of another. Originally, though, the word *scapegoat* meant an actual goat in Hebrew scripture—or so early biblical translators thought.

In Leviticus 16, the author describes rituals to be performed on Yom Kippur, or the Day of Atonement. These include sacrificing one of two goats, whose fates are decided by the casting of lots. One goat is sacrificed then and there, and the other is then symbolically laden with all the sins of the people, and sent out into the wilderness.

Problem was, when the sixteenth-century Englishman William Tyndale was working on his translation of this passage, he was stumped by the Hebrew word *'azazel,* used for the second goat. He surmised the writer must have meant *e'z ozel* ("goat that departs"), and coined the word *scapegoat* as its English equivalent. The translators of the King James Version followed suit, mentioning that a priest (in this case, Aaron) "shall cast lots upon the two goats; one lot for the Lord, and the other lot for the scapegoat. And Aaron shall bring the goat upon which the Lord's lot fell, and offer him for a sin offering. But the goat, on which the lot fell to be the scapegoat, shall be presented alive before the Lord, to make an atonement with him, and to let him go for a scapegoat into the wilderness."

Later scholars figured out that actually, *Azazel* must be a proper name for an "angry god" or demon (perhaps related to the Canaanite deity, *Aziz*), or the name of the place to which the second goat was sent.

(Actually, Tyndale turned out to be something of a scapegoat himself. A religious reformer determined to publish a Bible that the common people could understand, Tyndale was accused of heresy and forced into exile by the English Church in 1520. He did manage to publish the New Testament in English, as well as the Torah, or first five books of Hebrew scripture, as well as a few other Hebrew texts. But he was arrested and executed in 1536.)

SCIURINE

Pronounce it "SYE-yoo-ryne" or "SI-yoo-rin," but either way, *sciurine* is squirrelly. It means "pertaining to squirrels" and comes from the Greek word for this animal, *skiouros*. The Greek name is a combination of the Greek words *skia,* meaning "shadow," and *ouros,* meaning "tail"—the idea apparently being that the squirrel's tail appears big enough to provide the animal with its own shade. Various forms of this Greek name for the "shadow-tailed" animal found their way into Latin, then French, then English, first as *squirel* then finally, as *squirrel.*

Incidentally, the *skia* in *skiouros* is a relative of English *sciamachy*—a fancy synonym for "shadow-boxing," and the *ouros,* or "tail," is a linguistic relative of a several English words involving tails, including *arse.* See **ANTHURIUM**.

SCOMBROID

If you want to say that someone or something "looks like a mackerel," the word you want is *scombroid*. As Peter Novobatzky and Ammon Shea note their delightfully disparaging book *Insulting English,* "One day the occasion may well arise to insult a sallow, saucer-eyed, chinless, thick-lipped runt of a fellow. In this case, no other term will do." Indeed. This word derives from the term *skombros*, the Greeks' name for this fish known for the dark wavy markings on its back. These markings also inspired the sailors' proverb, "Mackerel sky, soon wet or dry," suggesting that when the sky is dappled with similar-looking, small clouds there will soon be a change in the weather. Such a cloud pattern also goes by the name *buttermilk sky*. Theoretically, you could also call it a *scombroid sky,* although then the proverb doesn't have quite the same ring to it.

SCORZONERA

The root vegetable *scorzonera*, which resembles a parsnip, has a "snake" in its name. The word comes from the Italian word for "poisonous snake," *scorzone,* and apparently alludes to this tuber's use as an antidote to snake venom. For the same reason, it's also called *viper's grass*.

SCROFULA See SCROFULOUS.

SCROFULOUS

The word *scrofulous* means "morally degenerate or corrupt" and contains the image of a little pig. It derives from *scrofula,* the name of a form of tuberculosis that affects the lymph glands, primarily those in the neck. Scrofula itself derives from the Late Latin *scrofulae,* which means "swelling of the glands," or literally "little pigs," from the Latin word *scrofa,* for sow. This name was likely reinforced by the fact that pigs are considered to be particular vulnerable to this disease. In any case, the notion of being similarly "diseased" inspired the use of *scrofulous* in a more abstract sense, meaning "tainted" or "lacking in morals," as in "What I can't understand is why in the world his constituents keep reelecting that scrofulous old snollygoster!" See SNOLLY-GOSTER.

SEPTENTRION

The word *septentrion* is a poetic word meaning "the north," which commemorates a team of seven oxen. The Romans likened the seven-star constellation *Ursa Major* to a team of seven oxen, sometimes referring to these stars as the *septentriones*—a combination of the words *septem* ("seven") and *triones* ("plough-oxen").

Because these stars were prominent in the North Sky, ancient writers such as Cicero employed the word *septentriones* figuratively to mean "the north" or "northern regions." By Chaucer's time, English speakers borrowed the Latinized version of this term and altered it to *septentrion* (pronounced "sep-TEN-tree-on"). William Shakespeare later put this word to fine use in *Henry VI Part 3,* when the Duke of York unleashes a torrent of angry insults, including "Thou art as opposite to every good, / As the Antipodes are unto us, / Or as the South to the Septentrion." Although now obsolete, the word *septentrion* remains in many dictionaries.

SHIH TZU See DANDELION.

SHREWD

The mouselike creature called a *shrew* has a nasty reputation for being dangerous and ill-tempered, and eventually this "sharpness" led to our word *shrewd*. These excitable, nervous little animals have been known to fight to the death over a piece of food, then eat their vanquished rival. It was once commonly believed that if a shrew skittered over a farm animal's back, the animal would be paralyzed, or *shrew-struck*.

Versions of this animal's name were around as early as A.D. 725, but by the thirteenth century, people were applying the word *shrew* to anything equally malignant or venomous—"a wicked man," for example, or more generally, "something exerting a bad influence." As happened with many other pejorative terms in English, people eventually began applying the word *shrew* to a specific kind of woman—a tempestous or nagging female (as in Shakespeare's *Taming of the Shrew*). The name of the shrew also gave rise to the verb to *shrew*—meaning "to curse"—and to the Middle English word *shrewd,* which means "cursed," or "wicked."

In fact, for centuries the adjective *shrewd* had a quite negative connotation; people used the word *shrewd* as a synonym for "depraved" or "wicked" or "malicious." In the sixteenth century, for example, a *shrewd child* was a naughty one, and a *shrewd cow* was ill-tempered. To *do a shrewd turn* meant "to do something harmful," and if you were sick in bed with a *shrewd fever,* you were suffering from a nasty one indeed.

Over time, *shrewd* also acquired the sense of "sharp" or "piercing." ("The night was shrewd and windy," Washington Irving once wrote.) Today we use the word *shrewd* primarily to describe a similarly "keen" mind or wit, and only a hint of the pugnacious little animal remains. (Incidentally, if ever you want to refer to a group of apes, it's properly called a *shrewdness* of apes. However, no one's been quite shrewd enough to figure out why this is so.)

SIMIAN

Pronounced "SIM-ee-un," this word describes anything reminiscent of monkeys or apes. *Simian* comes from the Latin word for ape, *simia*. (This word also appears in a medieval Latin quotation that is at least as relevant today as it was in the Middle Ages: *Exemplum de simia, quae, quando plus ascendit, plus apparent posteriora eius*. Or, roughly translated: "As with the ape, the higher one climbs, the more he reveals of his behind.")

SINGAPORE See DANDELION.

SINGH See DANDELION.

SLEUTH

The word *sleuth*, as in "a detective" or "intrepid investigator," is short for *sleuthhound*, a type of dog that has a keen sense of smell. Originally, these bloodhounds were used in Scotland for hunting game or tracking fugitives. Their name derives from the Old Norse *slōth*, meaning "animal track."

SMORGASBORD

The Swedes apparently saw a resemblance between geese and lumps of butter; the Swedish dialectal term for butter, *gås,* is a descendant of an Old Norse word for goose. The image of these bird-shaped butterballs later found its way into the Swedish term *smörgås,* meaning "bread and butter," or "open-face sandwich." Having added their word for table, *bord,* the Swedes came up with their name for a feast traditionally featuring sandwiches and other treats, *smörgåsbord.* This word has been around in English since at least the 1890s.

SNIPER

It's hard to sneak up on a *snipe,* considering that these long-billed birds are paludicolous (literally, "marsh-dwelling"), and are swift fliers. This means that hunters who shoot at such birds must do so from a considerable distance, usually while hiding on more solid ground. Thus in a very literal sense, the verb to *snipe* means "to pick off individuals by shooting from a concealed place," and led to our word *sniper,* which denotes someone who does exactly that. The verb to *snipe* has also acquired the more figurative meaning of "to carp," or "to make sly or cutting underhand remarks." Although the origin of this bird name is unclear, there are several parallel forms in Scandinavian and Germanic languages.

SNOLLYGOSTER

Although little used these days, the word *snollygoster* is an extremely handy one that denotes "an unscrupulous politician," as in "What a relief to know that the scrofulous old snollygoster can't run for another term!"

This political word may have a beastly origin: In parts of rural nineteenth-century America, parents used to keep unruly kids in line with warnings about the evil *snallygaster*, a monster that preyed at night on chickens and naughty children. Part bird, part reptile, the *snallygaster* struck with terrifying swiftness—hence its name, probably from the Pennsylvania Dutch words (*schnelle geeschter*) for "quick spirit."

Some linguistic authorities suspect an etymological link between *snallygaster* and *snollygoster*, a word that, according to the *Oxford English Dictionary*, applies most often, when it's applied at all, to "a shrewd, unprincipled person, esp. a politician." See BLATANT.

SOMMELIER

The *sommelier* in a restaurant oversees the establishment's wines and is usually quite knowledgeable about which wines best complement what foods. The origin of this employee's title isn't nearly so elegant, though: The Old French word *sommelier* means "an officer in charge of provisions," and more specifically, a "pack-animal driver." The word *sommelier* derives in turn from an older word, *sommier*, meaning "a beast of burden."

Sommelier is a linguistic relative of at least two other "beast of burden" words in English. One is *sumpter*, which is a name referring to "a pack horse, mule, or similar animal." Another is *summer*, meaning "a heavy horizontal beam supporting the girders or joists of a floor." This kind of *summer* is etymologically unrelated to the type of *summer* that is one of the seasons of the year. (Thus, contrary to any fun-in-the-sun images it might evoke, the word *breastsummer* is in fact an architectural term denoting "a horizontal beam that supports an exterior wall, and extends over an opening, such as a shop window.") For more "beast of burden" words, see EASEL.

SPANGHEW See TOADY.

STRUTHONIAN

Here's another word that really deserves more use, *struthonian*. It means "having a tendency to hide one's head in the sand (like an ostrich)." British writer Arthur Koestler coined it, playing on the word *struthious,* a more technical term that describes "anything pertaining to or resembling the ostrich." Since Koestler first coined the term *struthonian,* this word and variations of it have been picked up by others, such as the writer who noted a few years later: "A fine piece of *struthonianism* is the failure to accept the fact that teenagers are now in practice sexually active."

Struthious and its fanciful offspring derive from the ancient Greeks' word *strouthos,* which commonly meant "sparrow," or more generally, "bird." Incidentally, the Greek for ostrich was *strouthos ho megas,* or literally, "the bird that is big."

SUMPTER See SOMMELIER.

SWAN SONG

This term for "a farewell appearance or work" alludes to the ancient Greeks' mistaken belief that a swan remains silent throughout most of its life, then breaks that silence just before the moment of its death by singing a final song of unbelievable sweetness.

Although this lovely tradition apparently has no basis in fact, the idea has been embraced in several cultures. It's reflected, for example, in the German word *Schwanenlied,* which means the same thing. Apparently the German expression inspired the English equivalent, first used by Thomas Carlyle in 1831: "The Phoenix soars aloft . . . or, as now, she sinks, and with spheral swan-song immolates herself in flame."

SWEETNESS AND LIGHT

We have the curmudgeonly eighteenth-century English writer Jonathan Swift to thank for the phrase *sweetness and light,* which is actually a reference to bees. This phrase first appears in an essay he penned before writing *Gulliver's Travels,* addressing the question hotly debated in his time: Who has contributed more to culture and society—the ancients or the moderns?

In his essay, Swift likened his contemporaries to spiders, arguing that both have a poisonous bite and spin nothing but flimsy cobwebs that break apart or stay hidden in corners. In contrast, Swift argued, the ancients were like bees, producing both honey and wax, and "thus furnishing mankind with the two noblest things, which are *sweetness and light.*" For Swift, these bee products—the sweetness of honey and the light from beeswax candles—symbolized aesthetic and intellectual perfection. Therefore, he concluded, it was the ancients who had contributed far more to humanity than the moderns.

Some 165 years later, the British poet and critic Matthew Arnold helped popularize this phrase in his diatribe against Victorian materialism, *Culture and Anarchy.* Arnold contended that artists' quest for aesthetic and intellectual perfection made a key contribution to society, and he praised the ancients for "their ideal of beauty of *sweetness and light,* and a human nature complete on all its sides." Over time, this phrase lost its apian associations, and today we use the phrase *sweetness and light* when describing "someone or something pleasant and cheerful," often cloyingly so. See **APPIAN**.

TABITHA

The feminine name *Tabitha* comes from an Aramaic word that means "gazelle." This word's Greek equivalent is *Dorkas*, which gives us the feminine name *Dorcas*, mentioned in Acts 9:36: "Now there was at Joppa a certain disciple named Tabitha, which by interpretation is called Dorcas: this woman was full of good works and almsdeeds which she did." Dorcas was known for making garments for the poor, and the Book of Acts describes how she dies, but then is miraculously brought back to life by the Apostle Peter. Today the memory of this charitable woman is honored in the expression *Dorcas society*, which usually denotes "a group of church women who provide clothing for the poor." The earliest roots of the name *Dorcas* are reflected by the fact that the modern name *Dorcas* (or sometimes *Dorcas gazelle*) also applies to a type of small African gazelle.

TACKY

Originally, the word *tacky* meant "a small or inferior horse or pony." The first recorded mention of this word for the scrubby little horses found along the coast of the Southeastern United

States was in 1800 by William Tatham, an Englishman who chronicled his travels in a book called *Communications Concerning the Agriculture and Commerce of the United States of America*. In it he wrote, "You are thus asked (in local phrase and expression) to *truck* or *trade* for a horse, a cow, or a little *tackie,* etc. (which last term signifies a poney or little horse of low price)." Later this word also came to specify "a poor white farmer." By 1889, a book on the language of America defined *tacky* as a Southerners' term for "a jade of a horse; a sorry beast; and idiomatically a man neglectful of personal appearance."

As Craig Carver points out in *A History of English in Its Own Words,* by the turn of the century the term *tacky party* also entered the language, denoting "a costume party to which the guests came dressed as hayseeds and hillbillies, or in a later variation, dressed in clothes that were gaudy or lacking in taste, the prize going to the tackiest costume. (In 1911, future President Harry S Truman wrote to his wife: "I have a 'previous engagement' to go to a tacky party. I am going as I usually go when at home and I bet I take the cake. My very best friends would refuse to recognize me if they ever saw me in my farm rags.")

No one's sure how tacky originally came to mean "an inferior horse," although it may be connected with the use of the word *tack* as a term for "inferior food," as in the word *hardtack,* the name of a tasteless biscuit made of water and flour that was traditionally consumed on long voyages at sea.

Although its source is uncertain, it is clear that the word *tackey* eventually lost its *e*. Over time, the word *tacky* began to be used as an adjective meaning of "unfashionable," "dowdy," "shabby," "crass," or "vulgar." See **HACKNEYED**.

TARRAGON See RANKLE.

TAURINE

The adjective *taurine* describes something "characteristic of or resembling a bull." This word comes from the Latin word for "bull," *taurus,* as in the astrological sign of the same name. The Latin word *taurus* spawned several *taurine* words, including the Spanish word for bullfighter, *toreador,* as well as the name of the mythical monster of ancient Crete, the *Minotaur,* who had a bull's head and man's body, and lived in a labyrinth built at the behest of King Minos.

TAUPE

The name of that popular pantyhose color, *taupe,* comes directly from the French, in which *taupe* denotes that burrowing brown creature, the mole. The French word itself derives from the Latin name for this animal, *talpa.* The Latin *talpa* also burrowed inside the Italian word for mouse or rat, *topo,* which will be familiar to anyone old enough to remember Ed Sullivan's sometime sidekick, *Topo Gigio.*

TAXICAB See CAB.

TEAL

The bluish green color called *teal* was inspired by the same color on the head of the small, freshwater duck called a *teal.* Etymologists have traced the name for this bird back as far as its thirteenth-century synonym, *tele*.

TOADY

The word *toady* has a surprisingly stomach-turning history and has to do with the once-widespread belief that toads were poisonous. In the days before television infomericals, charlatans would hawk their cure-alls by having an assistant eat one of these supposedly poisonous amphibians (or at least pretend to). The assistant then collapsed into spectacular convulsions and dropped dead—only to be miraculously revived by the charlatan and his powerful potion.

First recorded in the early seventeenth century, the word *toad-eater* and its shortened form, *toady*, came to denote the sort of person so contemptibly subservient that he's willing to do something similarly disgusting at someone else's behest.

Speaking of toads, if you ever need a verb meaning "to cause a toad or frog to go flying into the air," the word you want is *spanghew*. According to the *Oxford English Dictionary*, the *spang* in spanghew apparently derives from a Scottish word meaning "to spring, leap, or throw," while the *hew* is of uncertain origin.

TODD

The name *Todd* comes from the Middle English word *tod*, which means "fox." In parts of England, the word *tod* remains a dialectal term for this animal, a *tod-hole* being a "foxhole," and a *tod-tyke* being "the offspring of a fox and a dog." See **TYKE**.

TOP DOG. See UNDERDOG.

TORII

A *torii* (pronounced TOR-ee-ee), is one of those decorative Japanese gateways or portals that resemble the Greek letter π. Often seen at the entrance to Shinto temples, these structures take their name from the Japanese word *tori*, which means "bird," and another word meaning "perch." (Thus *torii,* the plural of which is also *torii,* is an etymological relative of the word *yakitori,* which denotes a chicken dish with a name that literally means "grilled bird.")

TRAGEDY

The word *tragedy* arises from the ancient tradition of holding theatrical festivals at which the famous Greek plays were performed. It's fairly well established that the Greek ancestor of the word *tragedy* is *tragoidia,* which means "goat-song," from the words *tragos* (goat) and *ōidē* (song). Beyond this, however, it's unclear how the idea of a "goat-song" came to be associated with such dramatic performances. Etymologists have suggested several possibilities. One is that goatlike satyrs made up part of the Greek chorus in early tragedies. Another is that winners of the play competition would receive a goat as a prize. Still another is that these festivals were held in honor of the randy god Dionysius, who, in the Greek mind, was closely associated with these lusty animals. See **TRAGUS**.

TRAGUS

Ever wonder what to call that tiny flap of cartilage sticking out over the hole in your ear? Anatomists call this structure the *tragus* (TRAY-guss), a word that derives from the Greek word *tragos,* which means "goat." The reason: the hairs that grow at the site of this little fleshy projection, especially in old folks, resemble a tiny billy goat's whiskers. As in "Boy, Uncle Ned's tragus really lives up to its name!" And if you ever need to denote both such structures on Uncle Ned's head, the plural of tragus is *tragi.*

Of course, the tragus isn't the only body part that sports such a tuft of hair. In recent years, goatees have been all the rage. The name, of course, is a reference to the way this small growth of beard resembles a billy-goat's. See HIRCINE.

TREACLE

What Americans call molasses, the British call *treacle,* which is why the word *treacly* means "cloying or overly sentimental." However, the origin of treacle and treacly is hardly sweet. These words derive from the Greek word *thēr,* "wild beast," a linguistic cousin to the Latin word *ferus,* which means "wild," and still growls within such English words as *feral* and *fierce.*

From the ancient Greeks' word *thēr,* or "wild beast," came their word *thēriakē,* meaning "an antidote to a wild animal's poisonous bite."

By Chaucer's time, however, *thēriakē's* English descendant, *triacle,* had come to denote a type of foul-tasting medicinal antidote that could be used not only for venomous bites, but a variety of other ailments. Charlatans then began making these compounds more palatable by adding ingredients such as molasses.

By the late seventeenth century, a variant, the word *treacle,* had shifted to the sweetening agent itself.

TUXEDO

Wolves have left the faintest of linguistic footprints in the name of the article of formal attire called a *tuxedo.* This word's etymological history is full of surprising twists and turns.

It begins on the western shore of the Hudson River, which once was home to a subtribe of the Delawares. Other tribes referred to these people as the *P'tuksit,* a name that literally means "wolf-footed" or "round-footed." (Actually, this name was a scornful reference to the notion that the P'tuksit were "easily toppled" in warfare—that these "round-footed" ones were, in other words, "pushovers.")

Along came the English colonists who settled in P'tuksit territory and anglicized the name for this "wolf-footed" tribe, changing it to *Tucksito.* Eventually, they applied the name *Tucksito* to the part of New York State, and with a few linguistic alterations, the word *Tucksito* morphed into *Tuxedo.*

Now, here's where the formal attire comes in. By the early nineteenth century, this area had become a wealthy resort known as *Tuxedo Park.* There, in 1886, an heir to the Lorillard tobacco fortune caused a stir by attending the country club's annual ball dressed in a formal dinner jacket minus the traditional tails. This new style quickly caught on, and the *tuxedo* took its name from the site of its debut. Its lupine origins are now all but forgotten.

TYKE

These days we use the term *tyke* affectionately when referring to a small child, especially a little boy. Originally, however, the word *tyke* carried a far more contemptuous meaning, denoting an "ill-bred, worthless dog or mongrel." Over time, the meaning of *tyke* also applied to grown-ups, particularly men, considered "ill-mannered," "lazy," "boorish," or "mean." (In fact, in Scotland the word *tyke* still commonly applies to a "low, contemptible man.")

The word *tyke* later came to be applied "in playful reproof to a misbehaving child." When applied to a youngster today, "tyke" carries none of its early negative connotations.

UCHIWA

An *uchiwa,* as every fan of Japanese culture knows, is one of those flat, exceedingly lightweight hand-held fans. Pronounced "OO-chee-wah," the name of this manual air conditioner has a bird in it. The word *uchiwa* comes from the Japanese words *utsu,* which means "shake," and *ha,* which means "feather."

UKULELE

This stringed instrument takes its name from Hawaiian words that mean "jumping flea." The story goes that in the nineteenth century, a small, energetic British army officer named Edward Purvis played one at the court of King Kalakaua, and helped popularize this Portuguese instrument throughout the Hawaiian Islands.

Purvis was famed not only for his strikingly small stature, but because he played the instrument extremely energetically—so much so that the Hawaiians dubbed him '*ukulele,* from '*uku,* meaning "flea," and *lele,* "jumping." Over time, their nickname for the frenetic foreigner became synonymous with the diminutive instrument itself.

UNDERDOG

Like the term *hangdog,* our word *underdog* betrays a long tradition of inhumane treatment of dogs—in this case the grisly practice of pitting one dog against another in fights. The term *underdog* apparently originated in nineteenth-century America, where a dog with a record of victories in such brutal contests was billed as the *top dog,* while its opponent was known as the *underdog.* This word soon came to lend itself to more figurative applications, as when an 1892 newspaper article noted, "The mission of the Democratic Party is to fight for the under-dog."

Around the same time, the term *underdog*'s place in the language was reinforced by its use in a popular song called "The Under-Dog in the Fight." Written by, appropriately enough, one David Barker, the song included the lines: "I know that the world, that the great big world / Will never a moment stop / To see which dog may be in the fault, / But will shout for the dog on top. / But for me, I shall never pause to ask / Which dog may be in the right, / For my heart will beat, while it beats at all, / For the under dog in the fight." See **HANGDOG.**

URCHIN

Although today we tend to use the word *urchin* to mean "a mischievous youngster," or "a scamp," originally an *urchin* was a hedgehog. The word *urchin* wandered into English via the Old French word, *erichon,* which in turn arose from the Latin term for hedgehog, *ericius.*See **CAPRICE.**

By Shakespeare's day, people were also using the word *urchin* as a synonym for goblin or elf, as Shakespeare did in *The Merry Wives of Windsor.* Apparently this was due to a widespread belief that such spirits sometimes assumed the form of a hedgehog before carrying on their mischief. It wasn't that much of a linguistic leap for English speakers to start applying the word *urchin* to mischievous children as well. Over time, the term *hedgehog* prevailed over urchin as a name for the prickly animal, but its use as a term for a pint-sized human rascal remained.

Incidentally, the name of the *sea urchin* derives from an imagined resemblance between this spiny sea creature and the four-footed, terrestrial type of urchin. In fact, the *sea urchin,* has sometimes gone by the name *sea hedgehog,* as when one writer noted in 1602: "The Sea-hedge-hogge . . . is enclosed in a round shell, garded by an vtter skinne full of prickles, as the land Vrchin. [The sea hedge-hog . . . is enclosed in a round shell, guarded by an outer skin full of prickles, as the land urchin]."

URSA MAJOR See URSINE.

URSINE

The word *ursine* means "bearlike." It's from the Latin word for bear, *ursus,* which makes it a relative of the name *Ursula*—literally, "little she-bear"—as well as the she-bear in *Ursa Major,* the name of the constellation also called the *Great Bear.* See ARCTIC.

Incidentally, the Latin word for bear also appears in Linnaeus' original scientific name for the raccoon, *Ursus lotor*—literally, "washing bear," an allusion to the raccoon's habit of washing its food. The same image remains in the modern German name for the raccoon, *Waschbär.*

URSULA See URSINE.

URUGUAY

This country is named after the *Río Uruguay,* or Uruguay River. The river's name, in turn, was apparently inspired by one of two animals, although it's unclear which. The *Uruguay* takes its name either from *uruguä,* a Guaraní Indian word for a type of mussel, or from the Guaraní word *uru,* a variety of bird that lived along the river.

VACCINE

In the late eighteenth century, British physician Edward Jenner observed that women who worked as dairy maids rarely fell victim to the dreaded disease smallpox. Suspecting that this was because they had been exposed to the cowpox virus, Jenner made medical history by successfully using the cowpox virus to inoculate a patient against smallpox.

The medical name for cowpox is *variola vaccinia*. The Latin word *variola* means "pustule" or "pox," and derives from the Latin word *varius*—literally "speckled." (The Latin word *varius* is the source of our own word for "manifold" or "marked by diversity," *various*.) The *vaccinia* in the term *variola vaccinia* comes from a Latin word meaning "of cows." Because Jenner's experiment involved the use of cowpox, or *variola vaccinia,* people began using the word *vaccination* for such a preparation.

Its bovine origins make the word *vaccination* a linguistic relative of the words *vaquero* and *buckaroo*. See **BUCKAROO**.

VAQUERO See BUCKAROO.

VERMICELLI

Dig into a plate of *vermicelli* and you'll be eating "little worms"—from an etymological point of view, anyway. The source of this picturesque Italian pasta name is the Latin word *vermis*, or "worm," which has wriggled into several other English words, such as *vermiculture*, or "earthworm farming." This Latin word for worm also appears in our word *vermiform*, which describes anything "worm-shaped." It's most often used to describe that dingle-dangle of tissue at the end of the large intestine, the *vermiform appendix*. See VERMILION.

VERMIFORM See VERMICELLI.

VERMILION

Like *vermicelli* and *vermiform*, the word vermilion is a worm term. Its linguistic roots reflect the practice of crushing the berry-like bodies of female kermes insects in order to yield a deep red dye. During the Middle Ages, this insect went by the Latin name *vermiculus*—literally, "little worm," or "little grub." (For other English words colored by this method of making dye by making bugs die, see CRIMSON and INGRAIN.)

VESPERTILIAN

Here's a lovely word for describing anything that resembles or pertains to the flying mammal we call a *bat*. The word *vespertilian* derives from the Latin name for this leathery-winged creature, *vespertilio*, which in turn derives from the Latin word *vesper* for evening or evening star. The connection, of course, is that bats become active in early evening. (A similar idea may be reflected in the Danish name for this famously nocturnal creature, *aftenbakke,* or literally, "evening bat.")

Thus *vespertilian* is an etymological relative of a poetic flock of crepuscular words, including *vespers* (a religious service that takes place in the late afternoon or early evening), *vespertine* (occurring, pertaining to, or becoming active in the evening), and *vesper sparrow,* a North American bird so named for its habit of singing in the evening.

The adjective *vespertilian* can be used specifically to refer to these nocturnal animals, or in a figurative sense to describe someone who exhibits similar behavior, as in the 1911 story "The Glory of Clementina" by William John Locke: "As the studio was rigorously closed to him during the daylight hours, his visits were vespertilian." (See also BAT ONE'S EYES, which has to do with animals—but not bats.)

VESPINE

If you're looking for a fancy word for wasplike, there's always *vespine.* This term derives from the Latin word for wasp, *vespa,* which not only hatched our own word for the stinging insect, but also inspired the name of the popular Italian motorbike, the *Vespa.*

VET

We often hear the verb *to vet* in reference to the past of a political candidate or appointment. (As in "You'd think they would have discovered all of his shady sweetheart deals while vetting him for the job." Originally, though, the verb *to vet* meant "to subject an animal to a thorough veterinary examination or treatment." Today this verb refers to closely examining anyone or anything for errors, particularly when evaluating their suitability for some purpose.

The words *vet* and *veterinary* are linguistic relatives of the words *veteran* and *inveterate,* all of which go back to a prehistoric root that means "year." The word *veteran* comes from the Latin word *vetus,* which means "old" (literally, "having many years"), while the word *inveterate,* meaning "firmly established," or "deep-rooted," comes from a Latin word that means "to grow old." The words *veterinary* and *vet,* on the other hand, come from a related Latin word *veterinus,* which means "pertaining to cattle or to beasts of burden"—most likely because such animals weren't all that useful until they were at least a year old.

VIXEN

In the fourteenth century, speakers of English used the word *vixen* to mean "a female fox." It's a dialectal variation of the Middle English word *fixen* meaning "fox," which is itself an etymological relative of *fox.*

By the sixteenth century, the word *vixen* was also being used disparagingly toward women, denoting either a "female fox" or "a woman who is ill-tempered, quarrelsome, or shrewish." Shakespeare invoked this latter sense in *Midsummer Night's Dream*: "O when she's angry, she is keene and shrewd. She was a vixen when she went to schoole." See **SHREWD**.

As long as we're on the subject of vixens, here's another word you may need someday: *clicketing.* Although clicketing might sound like something you do at a computer keyboard, it actually denotes "the act of foxes copulating." The word may be an etymological relative of the verb to *clicket,* which means "to chatter"; etymologists suspect that the word *clicketing* may refer to the noise made by female foxes when they're clicketing. Then again, one sixteenth-century text on hunting suggests that the cry of a clicketing vixen is louder than mere chatter: "When a bytche foxe goeth on clycqueting . . . she cryeth with a hollow voyce like unto the howling of a madde dogge [When a bitch fox goes on clicketing . . . she cries with a hollow voice like unto the howling of a mad dog]."

VULPINE

The adjective *vulpine* means "foxlike." Because the fox has long enjoyed a reputation for being crafty and shrewd, the word *vulpine* also can be used to mean "cunning or sly like a fox." It derives from the Latin word for fox, *vulpex,* and is a distant relative of another fox word, *alopecia,* which means "baldness." See ALOPECIA.

WALLOP

Several hundred years ago, the verb *to wallop* meant "to gallop."
In the late fifteenth century, for example, William Caxton wrote,
"Cam there kyng charlemagn, as fast as his horse myghte walop
[Came there King Charlemagne, as fast as his horse might wallop]."
By the early eighteenth century, a poet would write, "witches
walop o'er to France, up in the air on my bony grey mare."

In fact, the words *wallop* and *gallop* are thought to share a common prehistoric root. However, *gallop* eventually overtook *wallop*
as the preferred term for "the fastest gait of a horse." Meanwhile,
as *wallop* began to lose its specifically equestrian associations, it
acquired more general meanings involving "loud and violent
motion." By the late sixteenth century, for example, *wallop* had
come to mean "boiling violently and noisily," as when one Lau-
rence Tomson wrote in 1579, "Oure affections boyle within vs, &
wallop, frothing as a seething pot [Our affections boil within us,
and wallop, frothing as a seething pot]." In 1863, Nathaniel
Hawthorne would use it in the same way: "We beheld an immense pot over the fire, surging and walloping with some kind of
a savory stew."

Along the way, wallop also acquired the meaning of "to lurch or move clumsily," as well as its modern sense of "to deliver a vigorous and forceful blow."

WILDERNESS

The *wilderness* is literally a "wild-animal" place, its name deriving from the linguistic predecessors of the English words *wild* and *deer,* plus the English suffix, *-ness.* The *wild deer* in this case, however, isn't necessarily of the Bambi variety. The word *deer*'s Old English predecessor, *dor,* meant any "wild animal," which is why it's uncertain exactly which animals Shakespeare meant in *King Lear* when he wrote of "mice and rats, and such small deer."

Over time, through the process of what linguists call specialization, the meaning of *deer* narrowed until it came to apply only to the cervine animal we think of today. Interestingly enough, though, the German cognate of *deer,* which is *Tier,* still retains its earlier, more general sense, which is why if you're headed for a zoo in Germany, you're going to a *Tiergarten*—literally, a "zoological garden"—where you'll see all kinds of animals that no longer live in the wilderness.

WOMBAT

Granted, the history of the word *wombat* isn't all that interesting. This name for a badger-sized, stocky, burrowing marsupial derives from a similar-sounding word in an indigeneous language of Australia.

But you may see much more of it in the form of a useful acronym now making its way around the Internet: WOMBAT stands for "Waste Of Money, Brains, And Time," as in "Oy, these marathon mid-afternoon meetings are always such a WOMBAT!"

X

The letter *X* evolved from the Phoenician symbol called *samekh,* which represents the *s* sound. The name *samekh* means "fish."

YAEL See JAEL.

YOKEL See JAY.

YONAH See JONAH.

YOSEMITE

Legend has it that in part of what is now California, an Awah-neechee chief named Tenaya was on his way to do some spear-fishing when he encountered a huge grizzly bear. After a bloody struggle, the hero single-handedly killed the bear with a tree limb and made the valley safe for his people. In honor of his mighty feat, they called their chief *uzumaiti,* or "grizzly bear." Eventually, this native word for grizzly bear was adapted into the name *Yosemite.*

ZE'EV

In Hebrew the word *Ze'ev*, or "wolf," doubles as a masculine name. Its feminine counterpart is the name *Zeeva*.

ZIPPORAH

The feminine name *Zipporah*, or *Zippy*, comes from a Hebrew bird word. In Hebrew scripture, this name means "bird," and perhaps more specifically a swallow or sparrow.

ZODIAC

The name of the *zodiac* derives from the Greek expression *zodiakos kyklos*, literally the "little-animals circle" or "circle of little beings"—a reference to the circle of little figures that make up its astrological signs. The roots of the word *zodiac* go back to a diminutive of the ancient Greek term *zōion*, meaning "animal." Indeed, most of the "little beings" in the zodiac are animals: Aries (a ram), Taurus (a bull), Gemini (twins), Cancer (a crab), Leo (a lion), Virgo (a virgin), Libra (a set of scales), Scorpio (a scorpion),

Sagittarius (an archer who is half-horse, half-human), Capricorn (a goat), Aquarius (water-bearer), and Pisces (fish).

The word *zodiac* is the etymological kin of such words as *zoology*, the study of animals. It's also a relative of *zoo* (short for *zoological garden*), and *zooaltry*, the worship of animals. A more distant relative of these words is the feminine name *Zoe*, a direct borrowing of an ancient Greek word for life.

ACKNOWLEDGMENTS

I'm grateful to Marian Lizzi for her *shrewd* (in the very best sense of the word) editing, to editorial assistant Julie Mente for her *apian* industriousness, and to copy editor Mara Lurie and her *aquiline* ability to spot errors. And permit me to *fawn* for a moment over Josh Kendall, who acquired this book in the first place. Here's hoping he doesn't feel like a *gobemouche*.

Thanks also to my agent, Russell Galen, for his always generous advice and counsel.

I'm grateful for the sustained writerly support and suggestions of Pamela Robin Brandt, Rory Evans, Robin Garr, Judith Newman, Susan Reigler, Katherine Russell Rich, Lindsy Van Gelder, and Mary Welp.

I'm fortunate to be related to a professional translator and a biblical scholar; thanks to Wayne Barnette and Henlee H. Barnette for their timely and thorough assistance. Researcher Janet L. Boyd also provided helpful and speedy sleuthing. I'm also grateful to the gearheads in my life—Alisa Perchick for continuing computer advice, Dave Harpe for getting funwords.com off the ground and into cyberspace, and Bill Rumsey for his help in setting up a database.

Thanks also to the following for various and sundry assistance:

Tim Ambrose, Mindy Badia, Harry Blumenthal, Joanna Goldstein, Cynthia and Brian Jones, Beverly Litsinger, Sally Marcum, Ernest M. Scheuer, Ten Wonderful Women, The Pearls, Val Scott, Amy Zink, Christa Zorn, and Mary Zriny.

Finally, adulation is due to Dr. Anne T. Nevils, DVM, who not only cared for my canine and feline companions—Luke, Raoul, Annie, Typo, Wylie, Fisa, Alice and Lloyd Bob—but cheerfully loaded me down with armfuls of veterinary books. And as always, thanks most of all to their other mom, my partner in life and love, Debra Clem.

SELECTED BIBLIOGRAPHY

American Heritage® Dictionary. CD-ROM. Boston: Houghton Mifflin, 2000. (Based on print version, *The American Heritage® Dictionary of the English Language*, Fourth Edition, 2000.)

Buck, Carl Darling. *A Dictionary of Selected Synonyms in the Principal Indo-European Languages.* Chicago: University of Chicago Press, 1988.

Carver, Craig. *A History of English in Its Own Words.* New York: Harper-Collins, 1991.

Crystal, David. *The Cambridge Encyclopedia of Language.* New York: Cambridge University Press, 1987.

The Eerdmans Bible Dictionary. Revision Ed. Allen C. Myers, Grand Rapids, Mich.: William B. Eerdmans Publishing Company, 1987.

Flexner, Stuart Berg. *I Hear America Talking.* New York: Simon and Schuster, 1976.

Gómez de Silva, Guido. *Elsevier's Concise Spanish Etymological Dictionary.* New York: Elsevier Science Publishing, 1985.

Hook, J. N. *Family Names.* New York: Macmillan, 1982.

Lewis, Charlton T., *A Latin Dictionary*. Oxford: Oxford University Press, 1987.

Liddell, Henry George, and Scott, Robert. *A Greek-English Lexicon*. 9th ed., 1985.

Novabatzky, Peter, and Shea, Ammon. *Depraved English*. New York: St. Martin's Press, 1999.

Oxford English Dictionary, Second Edition. CD-ROM. Oxford: Oxford University Press, 1994.

Random House Webster's Unabridged Dictionary. CD-ROM. New York: Random House, 1999.

Webster's Third New International Dictionary. CD-ROM. Springfield, Mass.: Merriam-Webster, 2000.

For further reading on animals and language:

Ammer, Christine. *Cool Cats, Top Dogs, and Other Beastly Expressions*. New York: Houghton Mifflin, 1999.

Lyman, Darrell. *Dictionary of Animal Words and Phrases*. New York: Jonathan David, 1994.

Macrone, Michael. *Animalogies*. New York: Doubleday, 1995.

Recommended Web sites for language lovers:

AFU & Urban Legends Archive, The—This site not only debunks internet hoaxes, but sets the record straight about linguistic urban legends, including the derivation of "posh" (which does *not* derive from "Port Out, Starboard Home") and whether the Chevy Nova really did sell badly in Spanish-speaking countries where "no va" means "doesn't go." (urbanlegends.com)

A.Word.A.Day—One of the most intriguing spots on the Net, AWAD was started by word enthusiast extraordinaire Anu Garg in 1994. It's now a thriving online community of more than 500,000 linguaphiles in 210 countries, many of whom discuss words on the site's lively chat boards. Features a free daily e-mail about words. (http://www.wordsmith.org/awad/index.html)

Bartleby.com: Great Books Online—Offering free access to *The American Heritage ® Dictionary, Fourth Edition*, this site also makes it easy to browse such reference books as *Barlett's Familiar Quotations, The Oxford Shakespeare, Strunk's Elements of Style, Gray's Anatomy*, and *Columbia Encyclopedia, Sixth Edition*.

Martha Barnette's Funwords—So, come by and see me! (funwords.com)

Maven's Archive, The—A lively collection of columns about etymology from language specialists at Random House, including many by Jesse Sheidlower. (http://www.randomhouse.com/wotd/index.pperl?action=dly_alph_arc&fn=word)

Merriam-Webster Online—Need to look up a word? The Merriam-Webster Collegiate Dictionary, 10th Edition, makes it easy. (m-w.com)

Richard Lederer's Verbivore—The Web site of the irrepressible linguist (a.k.a. "Conan the Grammarian") and author of such books as *Sleeping*

Dogs Don't Lay, offering a wide-ranging celebration of our marvelous native tongue. (verbivore.com)

Take Our Word For It—Melanie and Mike Crowley provide a wealth of easy-to-understand etymologies, plus a weekly word-origin e-mail that's accessible, accurate, and enjoyable. (takeourword.com)

Wilton's Word and Phrase Origins—Word enthusiast Dave Wilton offers fascinating word histories, along with a monthly newsletter for fellow logophiles. (wordorigins.org/index.htm)

Word Detective, The—The ever assiduous word-sleuth Evan Morris presents a popular weekly column on words and language—in a style that's at once knowledgeable and wryly funny. (word-detective.com)

World Wide Words—Extensive, thoughtful, and carefully researched etymologies by *Oxford English Dictionary* contributor Michael Quinion, featuring a popular, free weekly newsletter about language and more than 800 pages of online information about words, with an emphasis on British English. (worldwidewords.org)

yourDictionary.com—The most comprehensive resource on the net for language lovers, featuring a thoroughly researched and free e-mailed etymology each day. Highly recommended! (yourdictionary.com)